Advance Praise

Your inner critic is like a bad ex: relentless, toxic, and still living rent-free in your head. Tal Fagin shows you how to kick that asshole out, for good. This book is self-help for people who would rather die than read self-help, with candid, real-world advice that doesn't involve hugging crystals. Stop self-sabotaging and start living the life you deserve —because you don't suck, but your inner critic definitely does.

> Ellen Rapoport, writer, producer, director, and
> creator of the critically acclaimed comedy series *Minx*

This insightful and empowering guide helps high achievers transform their inner critic into an inner champion. With practical tools and mindset shifts, it shows readers how to overcome self-doubt and unlock their confidence, creativity, and potential. It is a must-read for anyone ready to conquer their biggest obstacles.

> Dan Kashman, founder and
> managing partner, Tenth Mountain

As someone who is always battling the negative voices within, as so many people do, I found Tal Fagin's down-to-earth wisdom, insights, personal story, and practical exercises for changing self-destructive thinking to be game-changing. Anyone with a tendency to be self-critical (which is pretty much all of us!) should read this book.

> Paula Derrow, editor of *Behind the Bedroom Door:*
> *Getting It, Giving It, Loving It, Missing It*

Sometimes I Think I Suck takes readers on an honest and relatable journey into the world of inner criticism. Through her own life story and the stories of others, Tal Fagin creates a powerful narrative that not only validates the "I suck" moments we all experience but also provides a path for change. The author's vulnerability resonates deeply, making her growth over the years feel authentic and achievable. Her insights help readers not only get to know and understand their inner critic but also begin to tame it with practical strategies.

Sunni Lampasso, PsyD, psychologist, leadership advisor, executive coach, and author of
Level Up Your Influence: A Self-Awareness Guide to Maximizing Your Growth and Unlocking Your Inner Leader

Tal Fagin confronts the universal challenge of self-criticism with refreshing honesty, warmth, and practical strategies. Through relatable stories and transformative insights, this book offers guidance that resonates on a deeply personal level. A must-read for anyone striving for clarity, confidence, and a more compassionate relationship with themselves.

Mary Beth Lawlor, publisher and editor-in-chief,
Happening in the Hills

Sometimes I Think I Suck is a modern-day yellow brick road, offering the reader a road map to a happier, healthier you. You will not have to walk the path alone, however; Tal will be with you every step of the way. Like a lamplighter, she illuminates teachings from psychology, mythology, neuroscience, and literature — and then shows you how to apply those lessons to everyday life. Consider this book your escape route from the people-pleasing, super-striving, self-denigrating behaviors that prevent you from actualizing your deepest dreams.

Lisa Matison Garrigues, author of *Writing Motherhood* and creator of Writing Womanhood

I have been working with Tal for almost two years, and she is an amazing life coach. I have struggled with my own self-critical, negative inner voice for as long as I can remember, and her teachings have helped me overcome many of these self-limiting thoughts and emotions. This book is an articulate and straightforward guide for anyone interested in well-being, providing concrete examples and exercises to overcome this negativity. Her personal story is inspiring and adds a welcome layer of authenticity to a topic that is, by definition, very personal for all of us.

Nirmal Roy, co-founder and managing director of Foundation Capital Partners, a real estate private equity firm

Understanding and confronting our inner critic is a crucial step in any healing journey, and this book offers an invaluable guide to doing just that. Tal provides a wealth of practical tips and exercises that make complex psychological concepts accessible, ensuring readers can genuinely engage with and understand the process of transforming self-criticism into self-compassion. As a therapist, I can confidently say this book will be a regular recommendation for clients seeking to evolve into healthier, happier versions of themselves. It's a must-read for anyone committed to personal growth and emotional well-being.

Stacey Blume Frankel, LMSW, ketamine-assisted
psychotherapist

What sets this self-help book apart is that Tal helped herself first. Part memoir, part advice column, part workbook, this book is for anyone who is looking to improve their inner dialogue with themselves and their outer dialogue with the world. Tal's ability to communicate how she broke out of old, tired, and unproductive behavior patterns will inspire you to do the same. Tal shares her struggles to "not suck" and then offers proven strategies from her training as a life coach to beat back the inner critic, find peace within and be more present. Believe me, she doesn't suck, and neither does this book!

Sarah Payne, certified Institute of Integrative
Nutrition health coach

If self-doubt has ever held you back, Tal Fagin's transformative book is exactly what you need. With compassion, humor, and a relatable voice, Tal shares effective strategies, powerful exercises, and personal stories to help you overcome self-sabotage and embrace the change you deserve. Each chapter offers actionable insights that will inspire and empower you. Tal knows these methods work—because she's lived them. If you're ready to rewrite your story and step into your full potential, this book will show you how!

Jamie Jackson Spannhake, health coach and author of *The Lawyer, The Lion, & The Laundry: Three Hours to Finding Your Calm in the Chaos*

Life coach Tal Fagin does a brilliant job weaving together personal stories and practical exercises to overcome our inner critics and embrace the goodness of who we are. Her words are a breath of fresh air for all the high achievers who find themselves stuck on a treadmill of unachievable goals and belligerent self-doubt. She moves us from fear to freedom, with some laughter and grace along the way.

Amy Julia Becker, author of *To Be Made Well, White Picket Fences, Small Talk,* and *A Good and Perfect Gift*

Tal Fagin's book is a heart-lifting two-for one! She convinces you to forgive yourself for all the years of not "getting it right" and then gives you the tools you need to break out of your ruts. Everything feels possible again. The only thing I feel sorry about now is my nearly empty highlighter!

Jim Kelly, owner of Kelly Law Offices

Tal Fagin's *Sometimes I Think I Suck* is a life-affirming book. It differs from other self-help books because it is both witty and smart. There are no charts, no endless rules, no preaching, and no empty promises. The author combines her story with a wealth of strategies to enhance anyone's life. Perfection is never the answer. The book is an engaging life lesson based on the author's experience as a life coach, lawyer, wife, and mother. It is a perfect book to be read and savored chapter by chapter. At its conclusion, one will experience a renewal and sense of self-worth that resonates in everyday life.

Maria B. Campbell, executive chairman,
Maria B. Campbell Associates

SOMETIMES I THINK I SUCK

Life-Changing Strategies for Self-Critical People

TAL FAGIN

HIGHLANDER
PRESS

ISBN: 978-1-956442-56-4
Ebook ISBN: 978-1-956442-57-1
Library of Congress Control Number: Applied For.

Published by Highlander Press
501 W. University Pkwy, Ste. B2
Baltimore, MD 21210

Cover design: Patricia Creedon
Author photo: Lora Noyes

Contents

For my parents, who are forever with me.

And for Rob, Layla, Michael, and Summer, my everything.

Author's Note

Your well-being is important to me. Helping people live their best lives is what I do. Before we jump in, however, there are a few housekeeping matters I'd like to address.

No book is a replacement for therapy, mental health services, or medical advice. Throughout this book, I offer strategies you can incorporate into your life to help you grow and prosper, but if you struggle with depression, anxiety, addiction, or any form of mental or physical illness, please see a doctor or a licensed therapist.

The ideas and experiences conveyed in these pages are my own, but the tools I teach and the practices I tout are not "mine." I did not invent them. Most of what I first learned, and later modified, came from author, life coach, and motivational speaker Martha Beck, PhD, when I took her life coach training course in 2014. Beck's ability to curate, adapt, and teach self-improvement techniques from a variety of sources—from Eastern philosophy to Dante's *Inferno* to modern neuroscience—continues to astound and inspire me, and I am forever indebted to her. I picked up other tools and approaches through additional classes and from my extensive reading and research over the years. The coaching field, by its nature, involves a tremendous amount of sharing and resharing of information, and I endeavor to give proper credit, whenever possible, to the appropriate sources. Any missed attributions are unintentional.

The tools I share are designed to be helpful to individuals from all walks and in all stages of life, but I also want to acknowledge that there is an inherent privilege in having the time and space to devote to these practices. If your schedule, responsibilities, or lifestyle prohibit you from taking the deepest of dives, please don't be discouraged. Simply do what you can. Even the smallest shifts can have tremendous impact.

What is said to me stays with me. The stories presented in this book are true, but all names and identifying details have been changed to protect my clients' privacy and confidentiality.

The exercises I've included here are the same ones I use with my individual clients and myself, but they won't work unless you actually *do* them. The more exercises you do, the more you'll benefit. Take your time with them, and please keep a notebook and pen handy as you proceed.

In these pages, I will reveal personal regrets, harsh self-judgments, and the methods I've discovered for turning self-criticism around to my advantage. As someone who places a premium on privacy, I am decidedly outside my comfort zone in disclosing these personal stories. I do it, however, to show how my life has changed for the better because of the practices I've adopted. How could I possibly justify keeping them to myself?

Introduction

 The most difficult times for many of us are the ones we give ourselves.

Pema Chodron

People can be so damn hard on themselves. If you are reading this book, chances are you know what I mean. You know that nagging voice in your head: the one that beats you up, puts you down, and drives you hard, second-guessing your decisions and questioning your abilities. The voice that zeroes in on your flaws but ignores your strengths—maybe even hurling insults—leaving you dispirited, confused, and full of self-loathing. The voice of *not there yet, not good enough, try harder, do better!*

Whether your negative self-talk is a subtle background whir you barely register or a piercing shriek you can't ignore, welcome to the club. As a life coach in practice for a decade, I specialize in self-critical people, and over the years, I've heard it all.

I'm not smart enough. I'm not thin enough. I'm terrible with money. I don't have the skills to apply for that position. No one cares what I think. My siblings don't respect me. I should be further along in my career by now. I can't be too ambitious, or people won't like me. I shouldn't be too outspoken, or I'll seem like a know-it-all. I'm too shy, too unfocused, too impatient, too old. I'm a terrible mother, a lousy father, a lazy shit. I should exercise more. Meditate more. Floss my teeth more. I should eat less. Drink less. Shop less. I should work harder, procrastinate less, spend more time with my kids. I should be more efficient, more organized, more productive, more kind. I am a loser, a jerk, a wimp, an asshole.

In other words, on some level, we all seem to believe we suck.

Some refer to these negative narratives as limiting beliefs. Others call them painful thoughts or disempowering stories or the voice of the inner critic. Whatever you choose to call them, know this: they are *not* helpful. You may believe, as many do, that this kind of negative self-talk is somehow motivating or productive, but it's not. It will hinder you in your career, undermine your relationships, and make it harder to achieve your goals. Even worse, it will diminish the joy and richness of this experience called life.

Over time, our self-directed critiques create a vicious cycle. We get stuck, like cars in a snowstorm, furiously spinning our wheels, expending our energy on our deficits while depriving ourselves (and others) of the gifts we could be sharing. We tell ourselves we can't pursue creative passions or professional goals. We miss out on opportunities to connect with loved ones. We commit daily acts of self-sabotage in lieu of self-care. We fail to fully inhabit our lucky lives.

We are, in short, our own worst enemies. But isn't it hard enough out there? Must we really make it even harder?

I believe there is a better way. A kinder, more compassionate way to relate to ourselves that is *also* more empowering and productive. That's why I wrote this book. This is the work I do with people and myself every day.

Clients come to me for reasons both personal and professional, seeking guidance and support, direction, and relief. Usually, they want to focus on the *outside* circumstances of their lives—advancing in their careers, improving their relationships, navigating big decisions, and managing stressors of all kinds. What quickly becomes apparent, however, is the root of the problem: their *inner* landscape and a pervasive sense of *not being good enough*.

Wherever they are in their lives—whatever they've accomplished or acquired—the satisfaction they crave eludes them. They focus more on their perceived problems than their many gifts, more on how things "should" be rather than how they *are*. As we explore further, another universal truth emerges: *nothing* ever feels like enough because *they* never feel like enough. When I look at these individuals, I see intelligence, warmth, creativity, and care. I see talent, resilience, humor, generosity, resourcefulness, and so much more. Unfortunately, this is not how they view themselves.

Very few of us do.

Instead of celebrating our talents, we lament our shortcomings, treating ourselves in ways we would never dream of treating other human beings. We subject ourselves to cruel insults, excessive blame, and a harsh tone. Often, the more accomplished we are, the more critical we can be. It's as if we believe that by taking ourselves to task for every little thing, we are doing ourselves a favor. But we're not.

As you may have guessed, I've also struggled to break free of self-criticism and the lashings of my unkind inner voice. In fact, my inner critic has been such a big part of my life that I've given her a name: Lola. When I left my first career as a lawyer to become a life coach, Lola shamed me, questioning my decision, and belittling my new pursuit, despite how vibrant and alive it made me feel. With Lola whispering in my ear, I felt weighed down and uncertain, determined to pursue my new passion but oddly hesitant at the same time. It was at this crucial crossroads in my own life that it hit me: if I was being held back by my own "I suck" stories, then, surely, others were too. Smart, influential, capable people, hesitant and unsure, restrained by insecure thoughts and faulty beliefs.

That's when I began to wonder: what would it be like if we all stopped listening to our Lolas? Imagine the exponential impact of all those caring, creative, and well-meaning people finding the security and confidence to bring their talents to the world instead of hiding them away, buried beneath a heap of insecurity, self-criticism, and shame.

I've written this book to help you—all of you strong and

thoughtful readers—identify and understand the ways you might be holding yourself back from flourishing, which certainly you are meant to do.

———

The truth is, learning to accept ourselves *as we are* is the key to true transformation. If you're rolling your eyes right now, that's okay. That was my first reaction too. Prior to coaching, I believed *acceptance* was just a euphemism for *settling*. Now I see it as the ultimate springboard. You see, underneath all that self-criticism is fear: Fear of exposure. Fear of rejection, failure, embarrassment, and the like. From that place, we are not functioning at our best. When we begin with acceptance, however, there is a calming effect on the nervous system that allows us to think more clearly and rationally. From there, there is no telling what we may do.

My own personal transformation and contentment has been hard-won. I have suffered great loss and struggled with uncertainty. I have felt confused, scared, and alone, then berated myself for "being weak." I have regretted past choices, then told myself to "buck up" and "stop whining." I have felt helpless and hopeless, lingering too long in toxic situations and unhealthy relationships, all the while believing I had to "power through." Worst of all, I have been the victim of my own unrealistic expectations and impossible demands, routinely sacrificing my happiness and well-being for the sake of achievement.

This hard-driving approach seemed helpful to me during my first career as a relentlessly ambitious corporate attorney at a global law firm. Back then, I measured my value through external accomplishments, those accomplishments—reviews, salary, prestige—being the only metric I knew for feeling good about myself. Except I didn't feel good. Enough never felt like enough. If I wasn't crushing it in some way, I was slacking. I was always determined to do *more*. To work *harder*. To look *better*. To go *further*. Whatever I achieved, I always had the sense that I wasn't *there* yet, that I *still sucked*. This mindset was such a way of life, I was barely aware of it. And to the extent I was, I viewed it more as a point of pride than a problem.

That was me spinning my wheels, expending lots of energy and going nowhere, constantly searching and striving but never arriving.

I had to learn the hard way that beating myself up was not the price I had to pay for accomplishment. Instead, using the tools we will explore throughout this book, I began to approach each day with awareness and intention, the kind of focus that energizes and sustains. That meant parting with my old "badass" tendencies and cultivating new habits. Now, rather than running myself ragged, I pause, slow down, and check in. I recognize when I am slipping into unhealthy patterns and take the time to question my "I suck" narrative, one painful thought at a time.

I'd like to support you in doing the same.

I am on your side. Think of me as your cheerleader, your compassionate friend, your faithful wingwoman. Think of me as your personal trainer, only instead of urging you to push harder or sweat more, I'm asking you to ease up on yourself. And I'm going to show you how. I will encourage you to define your goals, but also to consider the deeper motivations *beneath* those goals. And I will offer tools—simple, specific, actionable tools—to help you discover what it truly means to be satisfied with your life and, just as important, yourself. Because you definitely do not suck.

Believing that starts with the thoughts in your head. Using targeted exercises, I will encourage you to get up close and personal with the stories you tell yourself so you can uncover the ways you've been holding yourself back, whether through self-doubt, fear, inertia, or insecurity. Once you clarify and disrupt these *internal* obstacles, you'll uncover a wellspring of energy that will help you overcome any *external* obstacles you face. You will emerge feeling capable, invigorated, and empowered—fully equipped to live a life that doesn't suck. Not by a long shot.

And the great news? It's easier than you might think. Because once you learn, as so many clients have, to let go of your self-directed negativity and give yourself permission to feel more satisfied, whole, and worthy, you'll discover that much of what you truly want is already at your fingertips.

The practices that follow are expansive. They will help you develop presence and awareness and effectively manage challenging situations. They will allow you to regulate your reactions, improve communication skills, and deepen relationships. As a bonus, they just might boost your health, creativity, and productivity. Most important, they will help you recognize when your inner critic is on the scene and empower you to respond more effectively, rather than falling into unhelpful, fear-induced patterns—so you can proceed with more ease and confidence.

Let's get started.

ONE

From Lawyer to Life Coach: My Story

 Life isn't about finding yourself. Life is about creating yourself.

George Bernard Shaw

IN THE NEXT CHAPTER, WE ARE GOING TO EXPLORE YOUR PERSONAL "I suck" thoughts and get to know your inner critic a lot better. Before we do that, I'd like to tell you more about myself and my unlikely journey from lawyer to life coach. If you'd prefer to skip ahead and get right to work, please be my guest. Otherwise, here's my story.

Before I was a lawyer, I was a kid hell-bent on becoming a lawyer. Living my best life was always about making the grade, landing the job, earning beaucoup bucks. On a personal front, I just wanted to be well-liked and included, even popular. Proving myself, securing my financial and social status, and appearing impressive (even if I didn't feel that way inside) were my primary goals.

Back then, I would have scoffed at the strategies I suggest in this book. In fact, when I first entered Martha Beck's course in 2014, I *did* scoff. I was there to start a new career—and to succeed at that new career to boot. But my teachers and classmates seemed to be there for something else, something more; they kept talking about how *transformative* the experience would be, how much we would learn about ourselves, and how much lighter, freer, and more whole we would feel in the end. The symbol they used for all this growth was the butterfly. Apparently, I was a mere caterpillar on the brink of significant change.

At that, I rolled my eyes and let out a dismissive *Psssht!*

Maybe the *other* trainees needed to look within, challenge their beliefs, and shift their perspective, but as far as I was concerned, I was all good. I had already been through so much and had always coped, even thrived, despite adversity. To my way of thinking, I was a survivor who had fought through more than my fair share of trials and tribulations to arrive at what I thought was a happy, secure, and peaceful place. I didn't want to be transformed! I just wanted to get my certification and get to work helping others transform *their* lives.

So, I donned my armor, willing to listen and learn, but resolving to do so with care and discernment. I wouldn't buy in *too* much to these tools and mentalities, wouldn't blithely embrace what my teachers were presenting—not at first and definitely not all at once. Instead, I agreed to dip a toe in. Then I found myself wading in up to my knees. In the end, to my surprise, I dove in and took a nice long swim.

If you are feeling cynical or wary, I get it. Self-improvement has become big business. This highly profitable—yet not always entirely authentic—wellness industry can, at times, prey upon those at their most vulnerable. At the same time, you wouldn't have picked up this book if there weren't *something* nagging at you, right? I encourage you to keep an open mind to the possibility that there might be new ways to solve old problems. Perhaps you've heard the saying, "The definition of insanity is doing the same thing over and over again but expecting a different result." The quote is often attributed to Albert Einstein, who may or may not have actually said it. Either way, my clients often appreciate the reminder, as do I. It's always a good idea to experiment with new approaches as opposed to clinging to old attitudes and habits that aren't getting us what we want. To dip the toe, and then go knee-deep, and *maybe* even take a nice long swim. Besides, you have absolutely nothing to lose; you can take what you want from this experience and leave the rest behind.

None of us has all the answers, but I do know that personal growth and problem-solving are possible—*if* you're willing to stretch yourself, try new things, and possibly fail. The lawyer in me—a goal-oriented perfectionist who wields intellect, critical thinking, and practicality like weapons—has had to learn that lesson repeatedly. Over time, I have come to recognize how my previous mindset about career, life, and my place in the world could be rigid and limiting, helpful to a point but ultimately stifling. My new and current mindset, by contrast—which is kinder, more patient, and far more flexible—brings many more rewards. Shifting toward an open-ended willingness to keep reading and *just wait and see* might be the best thing you ever do for yourself. It was for me.

Growing up in the 1980s, I was my own helicopter parent. My parents were too preoccupied with their marital struggles to hover over me. They loved each other deeply but could not find a way to live together amicably. They divorced when I was nine, then proceeded to get back together and break up more times than I care to remember. The only thing more passionate than their reunions were the inevitable fights that split them apart. For me, it was like being on an endless roller coaster of breathless hope followed by crushing disappointment. No matter how many times they tried to "make things work," someone was always flying into a rage about something—usually money or the lack thereof—then walking out the door and slamming it shut.

Amid the chaos, disappointment, and failure, however, one constant remained: my parents' love for my brother and me. They had made a mess of their own lives, but we were their solace. Their pride in me was palpable. I was the bright star dependably shining in their storm.

I never wanted to jeopardize that status or disrupt any moments of peace while they lasted. So, for years, I assumed the burden of their happiness and became an expert in reading their moods. At home, I became adept at taking the temperature of any room I entered, tiptoeing through the fraught and twisted terrain of possible landmines threatening to blow up my family.

Along the way, I absorbed two major life lessons:

Financial security is a prerequisite to happiness. Without it, the whole house of cards can come crashing down. Translation: work hard, excel at school, pursue a lucrative, stable career, and always maintain your financial independence.

Love, family, and relationships are the most crucial things in life, but they are also complicated and fragile. So, love and be loved, but don't be too needy. Strive to be easy-going and pleasant, as well as mature and capable. Be caring and sensitive to the feelings of others, but always be able to fend for yourself. Translation: true love is unconditional…but don't trip any bombs.

It's no wonder, then, that I set my sights on law so early—in the fourth grade. Not only would it provide stability and financial security, but it seemed like something I could do *and* have ample time for a family. Whenever anyone questioned my certainty, I balked. *What did they know?* For as long as I can remember, I traveled a straight and narrow path toward success, guided by the feeling that I'd better not screw up, since even one misstep might prove disastrous.

My formula for success was straightforward: set a goal; identify the steps required to get from point A to point B; work hard; execute the steps in a deliberate, diligent, direct manner; achieve the goal; feel (momentarily) worthy and proud; then set a new, more challenging goal. And then…repeat.

For decades, this approach worked in my favor. It wasn't until years later, after getting everything I had always wanted and then losing everything I took for granted, that I felt compelled to reexamine my narrow view of success—and the childhood lessons driving my decisions.

Just after my freshman year of college, my father passed away suddenly. I remember sitting in the cemetery by his freshly dug grave, grief-stricken and bone-weary, my face puffy from crying. I had never doubted my father's adoration or devotion, but our relationship was complicated and often painful. He had "made so many mistakes," he always said, and was determined that I learn from them. Sometimes, his philosophy came across with tenderness—"I know I must have done something right in my life because God gave me you"—but mostly, he expressed his love by conveying life lessons meant to toughen me up. As I sat there on the ground, a few of his favorite expressions swirled through my mind: *Life isn't fair*; *the only person you can depend on is yourself*; *keep your head screwed on right*; and *stop crying before I give you something to cry about*.

In other words, taking the hits and soldiering on was the only viable choice. My father had little patience for whining or any show of weakness, and, at that moment, I promised him I would continue to make him proud. Suddenly, I felt he had been preparing me for this eventuality my entire life as if he had known he'd leave me early. I was shaken and stunned and indescribably sad, but I knew what he would want me to do. I stood up, wiped the dirt from my pants and the tears from my eyes, and resolved to blaze ahead, to make my mark on the world and forever honor his memory. Losing him made me more determined to secure my future.

For the next three years, I doubled down on my studies at the University of Michigan and got accepted into New York University School of Law, my top choice. I made the Law Review and secured multiple offers at top-tier firms.

I accomplished everything I'd set out to do, but it wasn't long before the whole carefully crafted plan began to unravel.

Corporate law fit me about as well as the excruciating high heels I wore while practicing it. The trappings of the job—the money, the prestige, and especially my brilliant, ambitious colleagues—were incredible. But spending my days drafting (and redrafting) contracts, conducting due diligence, and toiling over the minutiae of corporate transactions felt meaningless. Giving up nights and weekends to do it seemed ludicrous. I nailed my assignments, but I was uninspired by the work and unmoved by the mission.

And there I was, twenty-seven years old, a lifetime of plans and goals just barely realized, already smacked in the face with the one thing I had completely failed to consider: *How would it all feel?*

Questions I hadn't previously allowed began bubbling to the

surface: *What is the true measure of success? What is my real goal here? What do I want out of life?*

At the time, these pesky flickers from within seemed best ignored. *Who cares how you feel?* I scolded myself. *Get back to work!* With my mountain of law school debt and a mother I was determined to spoil after all she had done for me, I could not afford to indulge these questions. Instead, I remained hunched over my desk into the wee hours and turned up the dial on my determination.

Then my mother got sick.

She had a tumor. A malignant one. In less than a year, she was gone.

I was only twenty-eight, and nothing would ever be the same.

My mother's death left me feeling like a shadow of my former self—limp, frightened, and incomprehensibly alone. On the outside, I appeared unscathed, barely missing a beat at work, marching bravely onward. But inside, I was reeling, my stomach always twisted in knots and my heart newly prone to pounding fits of panic. Losing my father had been shocking but also carried a hint of inevitability. He had never made healthy choices. But my mother? Until her diagnosis, she had seemed invincible, the strongest woman I knew. Losing her was inconceivable. All my life, she was the one I could turn to for absolutely anything, whether I had something to celebrate, something to process, or something to grieve. She was my staunchest ally and greatest fan, the epitome of unconditional love and support. If my life had been a tightrope act, my mother had been my safety net. But it wasn't until I lost her that I came to appreciate how empowering that had been, knowing she'd be there to catch me if I stumbled and love me just the same. She was the secret source of my strength, and without her, I felt diminished.

And so, those smoldering embers of doubt grew hotter, until finally, a few years later, they burst into flames when I had a daughter of my own. Suddenly, the lessons from my childhood—*Financial success is the key to happiness! Never lean on anyone!*—felt like a burden rather than an anchor. As determined as I was to remain self-sufficient and independent, I also felt a great pull to put my family first. Just before getting pregnant with Layla, my first child, I had left corporate law, looking to do more personally meaningful work. I landed at the Queens County District Attorney's Office where I began prosecuting domestic violence cases. Rather than pulling all-nighters representing Fortune 500 companies, I spent my days fighting for justice in the service of women and children in abusive situations. I loved everything about my new job, but the hours caught me by surprise. I'd assumed my new position would afford me a better work-life balance, but it didn't, and that was before I had a child. As my maternity leave approached its end, the reality sunk in. If I returned to my job, I would rarely see my baby during waking hours. As terrified as I was at the prospect of step-ping off the career track, missing that time with my infant daughter terrified me more. I also knew how privileged I was to even have the option to stay home with her, which filled me with guilt and a particular strain of self-loathing I have since seen in many clients.

Yet when the time came to head back to the office, I couldn't do it. My mother had always worked because she had to, and I had always assumed I would do the same. But her death had changed everything. *Who knew how much time I had? How did I want to spend it? What did I want my legacy to be?*

And still, I struggled over my decision to stay home. I had been so invested in the image of myself as a steely career woman, had always considered my grit and work ethic to be among my most important attributes. But with my husband's encouragement and the flickers of doubt turning to a roar, I felt compelled, at least temporarily, to let that steely career woman go. *Work will always be there*, I told myself, shakily. My daughter's childhood would not.

And yet it felt like a betrayal. I had grown up in my mother's hair salon, watching as she stood on her feet day after day tending to a clientele that seemed to have it all too easy. My mother adored her clients and considered many of them to be good friends. I saw things differently. As kind and generous as they often were, I judged them. Harshly and unfairly. All these years later, it is still hard to admit that, but growing up, I couldn't help but compare them—these well-heeled, mostly nonworking women—with my industrious, breadwinning immigrant mom. I admired her so much more for her fortitude and independence. Meanwhile, all *she* wanted was for *me* to have the same opportunities and privileges enjoyed by their children, which she worked tirelessly to provide. My plan had been to work just as tirelessly so that one day, I could return the favor and take care of her.

Now my mother was gone, and I was giving up my career to stay home with Layla.

Suddenly, I felt less like the mother I admired and more like one of *them*.

Looking back, I am horrified by the assumptions I made about others based on their lifestyle or career choices. I was naïve and foolish and far too quick to make sweeping generalizations. Since then, I've learned that motherhood is one of the hardest, most challenging jobs there is, and damn important too. I am continually amazed by the women I meet and the depths and layers they possess, whether they work inside or outside the home.

But back then, I couldn't give these women a break—nor myself. Instead of settling into my choice and embracing the luxury of time and freedom with my baby, I remained conflicted and uneasy, and mired in "I suck" thinking. I only wish I'd had the tools to put those thoughts aside back then. But I just couldn't let myself be comfortable with it.

Or, rather, Lola wouldn't let me be comfortable with it.

Lola, as I mentioned earlier, is the name I have since given to my inner critic. And she was never more agitated as she was when I left law and before I became a life coach. She missed her power suits and her briefcase and even those excruciating heels. She could hardly stand the slower pace of mommy life. She was constantly pushing me to start a business or write a screenplay or volunteer more. But if I dared take any time away from Layla (and, later, my son, Michael, and younger daughter, Summer), she would judge me just as harshly. If I was racing, she scolded me to slow down. When I was relaxed, she told me I was getting lazy. Her agenda was all over the place, a maelstrom of impossible, contradictory demands I could never satisfy, that left me swirling in a perfect storm of insecurity and self-doubt.

At the time, I was convinced I was the only one plagued by a torturous inner critic, the only one marching along to the incessant beat of an "I suck" drum. It never occurred to me that anyone else (everyone else!) had their own harsh inner voices. I also didn't get that "she" was separate from "me" or that I could stand up to her abuse. Instead, like a kidnapping victim suffering from Stockholm syndrome, I was convinced I couldn't live without her. She was my drive, my motivation, my identity, and I took a lot of pride in "our" no-nonsense, ambitious, hard-driving approach to life, grateful that it had always allowed me to achieve so much.

That is, until I came to life coaching. That's when I realized how toxic and unnecessary Lola's presence truly was. Prior to that, I'd never heard of the inner critic or considered the pitfalls of my all-or-nothing approach to life. I hadn't encountered the concepts we will explore throughout this book, like negativity bias (the very human tendency to focus on the negative) or neuroplasticity (the brain's ability to form new neurons as we learn different ways of thinking and acting). I sensed a tug-of-war going on within myself, but I didn't have the language to name it or the skills to pursue a more self-compassionate approach. If I had, I imagine those early years of motherhood would have involved much less suffering.

Instead, I continued to struggle over my decision to stay home. *For years.* I felt conflicted, knowing it was a privilege my mother and millions of others simply did not have. And though I was grateful for my situation, I felt oddly oppressed by it too. And worse, I *hated* myself for feeling that way. Once all three children were in school full-time, I knew I wanted to work again, though not in the law. That's when my friend Pari, knowing I was casting about for something I could do within school hours, casually asked, "Have you ever thought about being a life coach?"

And then another friend asked the same thing. And another.

It wasn't a crazy question. I've always loved connecting with people on a deeper level, listening intently, asking pointed questions, and helping craft solutions to problems. At the DA's office, I bonded with witnesses, trying to help them outside the legal realm. More than once, my bureau chief gently scolded me, "Remember, you're the prosecutor, not the social worker." And in the years since leaving, I'd come to relish the intimate and personal conversations I had with other moms, where I could draw upon a softer, more compassionate version of myself as I helped people work through whatever challenges they might be facing. The more I thought about it, the more I realized that nothing lit me up quite the same way as listening to, engaging with, and helping others.

Have you ever thought about being a life coach?

My friend Sue, who had worked with a Martha Beck coach during a challenging phase in her own life, recommended Beck's course. After researching the program and speaking with a few coaches who had gone through it, I decided to give it a try.

Not that I did it wholeheartedly. Besides my skepticism about the entire enterprise, I was all too aware that life coaching didn't come with quite the same prestige as law. But I told myself that this was something I could do from home, something that would get me back to work almost immediately and entirely on my own schedule. Plus, the other coaches I spoke with were uniformly intelligent, kind, and caring women. Many of them, too, had left behind high-powered careers. As I heard them describe how much they loved their work, I felt an unexpected excitement rising in me.

In the years since, with the benefit of time, perspective, and regularly practicing the tools I share throughout these pages, I have finally found better balance.

This work has allowed me to drop my perfectionism and, instead, love myself better, to look beyond flip judgments to experience a greater truth. It has taught me to embrace a wider array of values—playfulness, warmth, devotion—and become far more patient and accepting. At the same time, it has allowed me to be more daring while also feeling more grounded and secure. It has led me to overcome long-held fears and take risks I would previously have avoided (or white-knuckled my way through). Now, I seek out opportunities, accept challenges, and make decisions of all kinds, not from a place of "should," but rather, from a place of excitement and interest.

Even more importantly, I can now experience the immeasurable benefits that *never came* with external achievement. I'm talking about the more elusive rewards I always unconsciously craved: contentment and satisfaction, a sense of home and comfort, new depths of confidence to pursue my dreams, and a profound sense of ease with how things *are*.

And I get to spend my days helping others find the relief and fulfillment they crave.

Not that I've given up skepticism entirely. Instead, I've learned to *use* it as a means of investigating further. Time and again, I've put these tools and tactics on trial and interrogated them under harsh courtroom lighting. And each time, my jury of one has found that they had quite a lot to offer. I bring all of this with me into my coaching. It's a real-world perspective that allows me to dig into people's struggles and problems and help them get *results*, though not always the results they think they are after. As I've seen again and again, the results we truly crave are rarely achieved by addressing external situations. The work we really need to do—at least initially—is on the inside.

TWO

Meet Your Lola

 The real difficulty is to overcome how you think about yourself.

Maya Angelou

IT'S IMPOSSIBLE TO SOLVE A PROBLEM YOU DON'T RECOGNIZE OR comprehend, which is why I believe that getting to know your inner critic is one of the healthiest, most liberating things you can do for yourself. It's not always easy. Inner critics like to operate in the shadows, pushing and pulling at us like some invisible puppet master. And bringing them out into the open can mean doing something that feels painful: honestly articulating your own personal "I suck" thoughts, the kind of brutal inner dialogue I hear from my clients every day.

One of them, Richard, routinely lamented his "lack of productivity," his "short fuse," and his "inability" to consistently follow through on personal goals around exercise. But the thing is, even when he was making progress, his inner critic slammed him for not having figured things out sooner or accomplishing more earlier in life. No matter what he did, it was never good enough for his inner critic.

Another client, Hope, felt she could never quite measure up to her business partner when it came to, well, just about everything. Hope's inner dialogue was rife with insults and accusations, such as *You're such a lightweight* and *You'd be nothing without her*—thoughts that left her feeling insecure and prone to behaving in a deferential, almost apologetic way toward the person who was supposed to be her equal partner. In our earliest sessions, Hope told me she felt "totally stuck" because, despite her misery, her business was "too lucrative to walk away from." Each time we spoke, she attributed her discontent to her partner, blaming her for "talking down" to her, "disrespecting" her, and "making her feel second-best." But before long, it was clear that Hope's inner critic was the one doing the vicious talking and condescending.

Or take Dr. K., a brilliant and stunning woman who seemed to have it all, at least on paper. A successful cardiologist with a thriving practice, she also had a solid marriage, a wide network of friends, a tight-knit family, and a passion for music, cooking, and entertaining. To be honest, she is the kind of woman I might have been jealous of in my former life, back when Lola, my own inner critic, had me constantly comparing and despairing.

Yet Dr. K. wasn't happy. Instead, she was overscheduled to the max. "I feel like I'm drowning," she told me, going on to say that she had "no time" for friends, for intimacy with her husband, or for "anything other than work." It may seem as if this were a function of circumstances—doctors have busy schedules—but it turns out that here, too, her inner critic was to blame. As we got to talking, Dr. K. revealed a lot about the belief system driving her to put so much pressure on herself. She seemed to believe that she "owed it to everyone" to be available, responsive, and helpful, and she lived by the credo "To whom much is given, much is required." In short, she felt utterly duty-bound to use her talent and her time to be a source of healing and support for others.

But guess what? That's not sustainable. Yet Dr. K., as harried and unhappy as she was, had never clarified or questioned the thoughts that drove her to show up for everyone else but herself. Even worse, all of this left her feeling incredibly guilty, or, as she put it to me, "I am such an asshole!" Not coincidentally, that harsh criticism cropped up whenever she considered prioritizing her own needs. As we carefully explored her self-critical thinking, Dr. K. realized how many of her daily actions were driven by "shoulds," "have-tos," and "cannots." As in: *I should always be available for my patients when they need me. I have to work these long hours because so many people depend on me. I can't reduce my schedule because that will put too great a load on my colleagues.*

As with all my clients, my goal was to help Dr. K. help herself—which started with examining the chatter in her head. Later on, I will share how we did that together—and the results of our efforts. For now, I'd like you to take a moment to think about all the ways *you* talk trash to yourself. What are the negative things you typically tell yourself? How do you put yourself down for your actions, choices, behaviors, or circumstances? And how does that make you feel?

It might be hard to answer these questions at first. Often, our inner critic's rants are so familiar, we barely notice them. Instead, we go about our days taking orders from this invisible presence without pushing back, unaware of the damage we do when we give in to their unreasonable demands.

What's ironic is that the first step in breaking free from this vicious cycle is to actually *listen* to your inner critic. What does it tend to say? And under what circumstances?

———

Exercise: List Your Greatest Hits

Breathe in and out for a few minutes until you start to feel relaxed. Next, recall a scenario where you fell short in some way or were disappointed in yourself or others. As you revisit the situation, think about some of the self-critical things that crop up in your mind, or that have in the past: What does the chatter in your head sound like? The brain is a master of energy conservation, so we tend to think the same thoughts over and over, as if there were a lazy DJ up there with a limited repertoire playing on repeat. What are your DJ's Greatest Hits—the familiar negative thoughts or personal stories that crop up over and over? One hint: often, they'll include the words "should," "shouldn't," "have to," or "can't," as in *I should be more organized; I shouldn't be so sensitive; I have to accept that dinner invitation, otherwise I'll offend someone; I can't say no to this project, my boss is depending on me.* Or sometimes they're even simpler, as in: *Loser!*

As harsh and judgy as these thoughts may be, try to avoid judging *yourself.* Remember: you are not your thoughts. Simply scan your mind and your memory and record whatever comes up, along with the tone you use with yourself. Once you've identified your personal Greatest Hits, list these words and phrases in your notebook.

———

Target Your Triggers

Now that you've got your negativity playlist, let's get even further acquainted with that voice in your head by looking at *how* and *when* it shows up. Bring to mind anything specific—situations, people, occasions, or activities—that gets your negative self-talk flowing or otherwise launches your inner critic into high gear.

Richard was triggered each time he "failed" to stick with a goal, as if each individual slipup somehow proved his overall incompetence. Hope, on the other hand, launched into despair every time she compared herself with her business partner. For Dr. K., simply waking up in the morning set her off, as did any situation in which she felt tempted to prioritize herself over others who might need her. Some clients are regularly provoked by specific people in their lives: mothers, fathers, siblings, certain colleagues, or particular friends. Others get triggered by specific activities, like attending a party, speaking up in a meeting, or paying the bills.

In fact, everyone I speak to seems to have a fraught relationship with money, whether they have too much or too little, they simply believe they don't manage it well, or they can't stop comparing themselves to others. Some clients tell me their inner critic gets activated whenever they experience a setback or make a mistake, whether personal or professional. Others tell me (and I identify with this) that it happens right after accomplishing a goal. Rather than celebrating, we diminish the achievement, chalking it up to luck or hard work, then moving the bar a notch higher. For many of us, the trigger is simply looking in the mirror.

———

Exercise: What Triggers Your Inner Critic?

Can you identify the who, what, when, and where of your inner critic? What really sets her off? Is it parenting? Finances? Anything you deem a failure? Is it specific people, certain activities, or even just a particular time or day of the week? Is it experiencing a "win" or a "defeat"? Most likely, you have various triggers, and knowing what they are and when to anticipate a reaction can only help, whether you choose to eliminate or avoid the trigger or better prepare yourself in advance. We will explore more about how to do this later. For now, we are simply aiming for awareness. Think of the specific things that get your negative self-talk flowing and write them down.

———

Reflect on Your Reactions

Next, I invite you to think about the real-life impact of your inner critic and how it causes you to react and feel. The challenge is to focus first on the physical sensations you experience, instead of defaulting to emotional labels like "afraid," "anxious," or "angry."

Some clients notice a gripping in the belly, a furrowing of the face and brow, or a clenching of the jaw. One describes a heavy, suffocating pressure she calls "bricks on my boobs" that takes over whenever she is feeling overwhelmed. Many others, often those who have trouble speaking up or expressing themselves, describe a knotted sensation in the throat.

As we proceed through this book, you'll learn to recognize how *your* body alerts you to the presence of your inner critic. You will also come to see how wise and trustworthy the physical body can be, especially compared with your frightened, worried mind. For now, let's practice identifying one of your painful thoughts while scanning your body and noticing exactly what this thought causes you to experience physically. Beyond the physical sensation, identify what your negative self-talk leads you to do or prevents you from doing. When you are in this charged state, do you curl up in a ball and hide from the world? Do you get deflated or fired up? Do you become overly cautious or highly aggressive?

Some people feel sorry for themselves or hurl blame on others. They might pick fights, get resentful or pushy, procrastinate, gossip, or become judgmental. Some people push themselves too hard, neglecting basic needs and thrusting themselves into overdrive. (That's me!) Others shut down entirely and climb into bed. Some get loud or forceful, while others make themselves small and meek. I know people who get overcontrolling, and others who go into chameleon mode, conforming to what they think others expect of them. And some turn to potentially self-sabotaging forms of coping such as comfort eating, losing hours on social media, or escaping through alcohol, drugs, or shopping.

Now, it's your turn. Do the exercise below, trying to identify both your internal and external reactions to your critical voice. Make sure to notice both direct and indirect behaviors, whether toward yourself or others, such as getting aggressive or avoidant (direct) or creating cruel, judgmental narratives in your mind (indirect). Take this opportunity to fully experience the impact your critic has in your life.

―――

Exercise: Identify Your Critical Reactions

Pick an item from your Greatest Hits list. Next, close your eyes, sit back, relax, and breathe deeply. Imagine a scenario where you are being hard on yourself, where you are really holding on to (and believing) whatever harsh story you typically tell yourself. For example, *You should be more successful by now*, or *You are such a coward*, or *You look hideous today*. Whatever your critical thought is, hold it in your mind, believe it to be true, and dwell on it for a full minute if you can, staying in that place of self-judgment and self-criticism.

Notice how you react, specifically paying attention to what you're feeling in your body.

Beyond the physical sensations, note other times you've had this thought and your habitual resulting behaviors. What does this negative self-talk cause you to do or not do? How does your negativity cause you to treat other people in your orbit? How does it cause you to treat yourself?

What, if anything, has it cost you in your life?
Be patient here. These questions are intended to help you clarify and comprehend the full impact of your negative thinking—on your emotional state, your behavior, and your relationships. Reflecting this way can be a really difficult, but also profound, experience. And rest assured, we will be moving along to some helpful tools to confront and change these self-criticisms and the negative feelings they evoke.

―――

Whatever difficult feelings you experienced during this exercise, I assure you you're not alone. Over the years, I have heard—and felt

—them all. But once I slowed down enough to really listen to the way I spoke to myself, then connected that inner dialogue to the emotions, energy level, and behavior that followed, that's when things really started to change for me. I had spent years living *in reaction* to Lola's rants but had never taken the time to appreciate the toll that had taken on me or those around me. It was as if I had been unwittingly carrying an invisible backpack full of stones and had finally allowed myself to put it down. That's when I began living my life in a whole new way—lighter, calmer, and more authentic. Happier and more confident. Braver and more content.

This is what I want for you, too.

THREE

What Truly Matters

 The simple things are also the most extraordinary things, and only the wise can see them.

Paulo Coelho, *The Alchemist*

NOW THAT YOU'VE GOTTEN TO KNOW YOUR INNER CRITIC A LITTLE bit, I'd like to ask you to take a step back and look at your life in a broader way. To help get you there, I'll start by asking you a few questions:

- Why did you pick up this book?
- What facets of your life do you wish were different?
- In what areas do you find yourself being self-critical, feeling stymied, or believing you suck?

If there is one thing I've noticed lately, it's how easy it is for us to operate on autopilot. We pursue degrees, relationships, and career opportunities without ever stopping to consider what we *truly* want or *why* we want it. We do the same when it comes to our daily activities, interactions, and routines. Oftentimes, the inner critic has a role to play here, keeping us in thrall to habits and behaviors that don't serve us well. My goal for you is to be more deliberate about how you live your life, and more thoughtful and intentional about your pursuits and the deeper motivations that drive you. I know you are busy, and the pull of obligations is powerful. But please consider this a friendly invitation to pause—I am going to say that a lot—and think about how you *actually* want to live, as opposed to what you "should" want or "have to" do.

Perhaps you want to take your career to the next level or switch paths altogether. Maybe you want to reduce stress, increase fitness or generally enhance your health or appearance. Or maybe you yearn for more intimacy with your spouse, more connection with your children, more appreciation from your family? Maybe you are struggling to find new love, or coping with loss or a difficult transition, or feel stuck in a bad situation or relationship. Maybe, like so many of us, you feel generally overwhelmed and burdened by responsibilities and are seeking a greater sense of balance.

Or perhaps you simply feel that something is amiss, but you aren't sure what it is. Everything might look good on paper, and you're getting by, but for some mysterious reason, you don't feel truly alive. You sense you could be happier overall but have no idea where or how to start.

I talk to so many people yearning for so much. All of the above, really. Wherever they are in life, they want to be somewhere else. And they want me to tell them what to do and how to get there.

Perhaps you can relate?

If I could wave a wand and fix everything for them—and for you—I would. But coaching is not about quick fixes. It is a process intended to help you get from here to there on your own. My job is to create a safe and trusting space, to listen deeply and ask the kinds of questions that guide people toward their own answers. Which is why, as we move forward together, I will be asking you to pause and reflect, to be still, introspective, and honest before you attempt to answer the questions I am asking. When you allow yourself to pause and be still, you're apt to uncover a whole other set of longings: for satisfaction and contentment, for safety and belonging, for validity and love. In the quiet moments, when we tune out all the noise in life that tends to lead us astray, most of us instinctively know what we truly need and want.

With my clients, I can tell when we are getting close to those essential wants and needs when they tell me, usually along with a massive exhale, what it is they *just* want.

I just want to relax. I just want to feel comfortable in my own skin. I just want to stop fighting. When will I ever be able to just be? These breathy declarations of *just*, I've discovered, almost always come with a sense of relief. They provide clues to what might make us feel more whole and content and are also key to helping us access our simplest, most essential desires. It's as if we use the word *just* to say, *If this is all I got, it would be enough.* How interesting, then, that the word *just* is also the root of the Latin *justus*, meaning "lawful, rightful, true," and also "proper, perfect, complete, reasonable, suitable, sufficient, right."[1]

So many of us have been conditioned to strive and strategize, to focus on the external markers of what makes a successful life, rather than focusing on what we instinctively crave. But by slowing down and identifying what you *just* want, you'll discover a safe place to rest and reset. I think of *just want* as the opposite of "I suck." The former brings a profound sense of relief and simple acceptance, or an honest statement of aspiration. The latter is a place of despair.

So…what simple yet extraordinary things do you yearn for most? What is it that you *just* want?

If you aren't quite sure (and many people aren't), let's take some time to check in and see what we might uncover.

———

Exercise: Dream Day

A key component of silencing self-criticism and transforming your life for the better is taking the time to reflect on your most essential desires. To do that, I'd like you to luxuriate in a dreamier version of your life. After all, it's always easier to get somewhere when you have a clear picture of your destination. This exercise, which combines a journaling ritual I've used all my life with a similar "ideal day" tool from my coach training, will help you access your true intentions, reveal your ideals, and surface your hidden desires.

Start by setting aside some time, ideally twenty or thirty minutes. Find a quiet, comfortable, private place to sit, where you won't be interrupted. Make sure your notebook and pen are nearby, then close your eyes and take a few deep breaths to settle yourself. Next, conjure up a dreamy, near-perfect day. Your Dream Day can lean toward the realistic, as you envision a more ideal, *just right* version of a typical day in your life, or you can let your imagination roam toward the fantastical. It can be a workday, a playday, or a combination. In short, it can be whatever you'd like it to be.

Picture your fantasy day from start to finish, from the moment you wake up until you drift off to sleep. Or, if you prefer, zero in on a more specific time, place, activity, or encounter. In each case, allow your vision to unfold organically as opposed to thinking about "shoulds" or "musts." Who are you with, if anyone? Where do you go? What do you do, or not do? How do you feel? As you mentally move through each hour, focus on the details: the sights and sounds, your surroundings and activities, the presence or absence of others, and whatever sensory experiences or emotions you notice.

Dwell there.

After enjoying some time in your dreamy day, grab your notebook and write about your vision, reliving and describing the experience and your feelings in the present tense. *I wake up early after a restful sleep. I smile as I smell coffee brewing in the kitchen. My husband is still asleep beside me, and I slide over to snuggle. The sun is just coming up, and I feel calm, yet excited to tackle the day ahead. I roll out my yoga mat by the window, grateful for the spectacular ocean view....*

Your vision is only for you, and there are no parameters. You can be anywhere in the world, living any way you like, whether grand or simple. Even time can be suspended. Just close your eyes and let it be.

————

Hopefully, you took your time with that exercise and allowed yourself to enjoy it. Notice if anything surprised you—whether your surroundings, your chosen activities, or the company you kept. Consider repeating the exercise on separate occasions, as often as you like. I make it a point to do this Dream Day exercise at least once a year, and each time, I find it revelatory. Last year, I was surprised to find myself zipping around town in an electric-blue Jeep, a vehicle I had never owned or even considered owning. One client, Brody, a self-described "country boy," delighted in finding himself living in a gleaming, modern high-rise apartment overlooking Manhattan. I still don't own a Jeep, but the way I felt in that vision—youthful, adventurous, and carefree—helped me see that I was taking my role as "mommy" a bit too seriously at that time, and it provided motivation to shake things up more often. Brody hasn't moved to the big city, but this exercise helped him realize he wanted to "get out of Dodge" more often. I've had clients come to see that they are happier than they realized within a marriage (or that they are ready to leave). Some have found a new sense of purpose in a career they thought had run its course, while others discovered an eagerness to explore something entirely new.

Whatever you noticed about your fantasy day, think about what it might mean or represent. What is your vision trying to tell you? Is there something you are longing to feel more or less of, and are there any small changes you can make to help bring about that dreamy feeling?

Now, I'll ask you to return to the questions I asked you at the beginning of this chapter, plus a few others. Why? To help you clarify your reason for being here with me and what you hope to achieve.

Give yourself a moment to be still and quiet, to pause. Next, take three deep, deliberate breaths, letting your lungs fill with each inhalation, then emptying them completely with each exhalation. Pick up your notebook and pen and reflect on where you are in your life currently, including your career, home life, health, relationships, regrets—whatever comes to mind. You don't need to get very specific. Simply write down whatever comes up as you answer the following questions:

1. Why did you pick up this book?
2. What are your areas of discontent? What facets of your life do you wish were somehow different or improved, and how so?
3. By contrast, what aspects of your life make you feel proud or passionate or pleased?
4. What do you want more of in your life? What would you like less of? What makes you…happy?

If that feels like too many questions at the moment, pick just one or two that speak to you, then take your time, letting your mind and pen flow without judgment or editing. The more vulnerable and honest you can be, the better.

If you feel impatient with this exercise, know that stopping to ask "why?" is one of the most important habits you can develop in your effort to clarify what you truly desire. It can also prove invaluable as you endeavor to root out your inner critic. I make it a point to pause frequently, on a daily basis, and ask myself why. I encourage my clients to do the same.

"Why?" is such a simple question, but one with a lot of power. It helps us drill down to the essence of things, be they values, aspirations, or attitudes. Whatever *whys* we discover can keep us motivated and enthusiastic, focused and engaged. Personal growth can be difficult, but clarifying your motivations can help anchor you when things get rough or you want to give up. Beyond that, knowing your *whys* can transform difficult or dull, even dreaded, tasks into far more worthwhile endeavors. For instance, when I was toiling away at the law firm late into the night, my *whys*—being a team player, serving the firm and its clients to the best of my ability, earning my keep—helped make isolated assignments feel less onerous. These days, I might stop to ask myself why I am doing a mundane chore such as folding the laundry. Suddenly, this routine activity feels like an act of love—a way of caring for my family. By asking "why?" I can reframe and shift my laundry experience, and the same goes for countless things we all do daily, from hitting the gym to volunteering our time to putting in the extra effort at the office.

Asking "why?" invites us to feel empowered, illuminating the intentionality and purpose underlying our various choices. From there, it is easier to act deliberately, from a place of authentic interest, as opposed to acting out of fear, obligation, or mindless habit. But the power of asking "why?" extends far beyond anchoring us in our motivations. It can also ground you in the present, keeping you mindful and aware instead of proceeding thoughtlessly through your days. When you reach a moment of difficulty—whenever you're feeling insecure, upset, lost, angry, stuck, or woeful—pausing to ask "why?" can provide insights that would otherwise remain hidden to you. As we saw in Chapter Two, your "I suck" thoughts have an impact. When your inner critic is on the scene, you experience both physical and behavioral ramifications. It may start with a stomachache or a sense of heat rising throughout your body. Maybe you get short-tempered. Maybe you become avoidant or silence yourself. Whatever your personal pattern, practice paying attention to it. As unpleasant as these situations may be, they are also a golden opportunity to pause and ask "why?"

One client, Steve, recently told me that he lives with a near-constant feeling of low-grade tension and worry. The feeling, which Steve described as "full-body tightness, plus butterflies, plus fatigue," had been there so long, he assumed he would never be rid of it. "It's just part of who I am," Steve said. "Like it's in my DNA."

When I asked Steve to practice questioning the feeling—to make it a point to notice whenever it surfaced and then stop to ask himself *why* it might be there—things got very interesting.

Steve realized how often he lived in a state of anticipation, bracing himself for "trainwrecks in the making" even during pleasant, nonthreatening situations. He also realized how often he avoided social situations (or suffered through them in a state of alertness and mistrust).

Again, I asked Steve why he felt this way. Who was out to hurt him? When was the last time he was slammed by a "trainwreck"?

Ultimately, Steve grasped how deeply he believed that his worrying was keeping him safe, causing him to be extra vigilant about people and situations that might cause him pain or embarrassment. But when I inquired further, Steve could not identify anyone, or any recent event, that justified his stance. He also realized how long he had lived under the weight of that belief, even though he had never articulated it before.

Bringing this unspoken shadow belief to the surface allowed us to explore even further, to look at the reality of Steve's life (where there were hardly any bad actors or trainwrecks at all), and, finally, to let Steve let go of some of his habitual tension.

Steve's story is a common one. It exemplifies how, all too often, we attribute our difficulties to some situation or circumstance when it's merely the pulling and straining of our inner thoughts—self-critical or otherwise—twisting and turning beneath the surface, that is the real culprit.

But when you take the time to pause and check in, to observe and clarify your thinking, new possibilities open up.

———

Exercise: Practice Asking "Why?"

Over the next few days, be intentional about stopping to ask yourself why. Whether you find yourself feeling tired or sluggish, elated or jovial, cranky, impatient, or anything else, practice pausing and investigating that feeling state. Is it connected to a particular task or some story you are telling yourself? In my case, I always thought it was the act of doing laundry that left me feeling irritated and annoyed. Stopping to ask myself why, however, revealed a whole new world of insight. Beyond your moods, you might also want to practice questioning physical sensations or any experience of reactivity. Why is your neck tight or your heart rate elevated? Why does the mess in your daughter's bedroom have you so agitated? Is it the circumstances at play, or something deeper? Are you equating that mess with disrespect or laziness or some other character flaw, as opposed to *just* a messy room?

It is all too easy for most of us to operate in a mindless, unaware state. Easy, but not helpful, as we'll explore in the next chapter. That is why I will be asking you to do a lot of this type of pausing and questioning. Not only will it help you be more present and thoughtful as you move through your days, but it will also help you cultivate the kind of awareness required to combat self-critical thinking.

———

FOUR

Introducing Thinking Twice
and the Four Cs

 The greatest weapon against stress is our ability to choose one thought over another.

William James

IT'S EASY TO BELIEVE THAT OUR LIVES' EXTERNALITIES DETERMINE our happiness. We focus on facts and circumstances—our financial status, career or relationship satisfaction, even the weather—and let these drive our moods and inform our sense of how we are faring in life. And these things *do* matter, of course, as do biological factors and brain chemistry. But our *thoughts*—including how we perceive, interpret, and judge the world around us—have far more influence on how we feel and what we do than most of us realize. Ditto for the way we judge ourselves.

When I first trained to be a life coach, this concept seemed ridiculous, even offensive. My instructors expected me to believe that it wasn't the sorry facts of my life determining how I felt, but rather, the way I "perceived" them? *Yeah, right!* As someone who had been devastated by the early loss of both parents, I was adamant that circumstances caused my pain and suffering. My parents were dead, and I missed them. The tragedy I experienced had nothing to do with the stories in my head.

I had a lot to learn.

By some estimates, the average person has approximately 6,000 thoughts per day.[2] Others put the number closer to 70,000.[3] Either way, that's a lot of thinking! It starts as soon as we wake up and persists throughout the day. Thought snippets or entire stories—mundane, morose, or merely distracting—float through our minds. *I can't afford that. I'll never meet anyone. My colleagues aren't pulling their weight. I am too old for this. Must buy toilet paper!* These thoughts trigger both feelings and behavior, creating self-perpetuating cycles that can decrease the quality of our lives.

In the case of "I suck" thinking, they can also weigh us down and keep us stuck, which is why watching your thoughts and learning to redirect them—Thinking Twice—is so crucial.

In *The How of Happiness: A Scientific Approach to Getting the Life You Want,* author and psychology professor Sonja Lyubomirsky introduces the 50-40-10 rule of happiness. Essentially, she posits that fifty percent of our happiness depends on genetics and is fixed. This is known as the happiness set point, and it tends to stay pretty much the same over time no matter what happens to us. Lyubomirsky goes on to explain that forty percent of our happiness is tied to our thinking and behavior alone, while only ten percent has to do with outside circumstances. Only ten percent! Translation: all the things we think dictate happiness—whether we are married or divorced, wealthy or poor, stunning or homely—count for very little and rarely have a lasting impact.

As for the forty percent under our control, "intentional, effortful activities have a powerful effect on how happy we are, *over and above the effects of our set points and the circumstances in which we find ourselves,*" Lyubomirsky writes.[4] "If an unhappy person wants to experience interest, enthusiasm, contentment, peace, and joy, he or she can make it happen by learning the habits of a happy person."[5]

One habit Lyubomirsky highlights is the way that happy people tend to *avoid overthinking* and *routinely make the choice to feel optimism or self-efficacy regarding one's life* (emphasis added). By contrast, our tendencies toward negative thinking often make life harder than necessary. The good news is that changing our patterns of thought and the way we interpret life events is possible and can have a powerful influence over how we feel about ourselves and about life.

For example, picture yourself waking up on a sunny summer Sunday, well-rested and excited for the day. Maybe you'll play tennis, ride your bike, or relax with a good book. Later, you plan to meet friends for a lakeside picnic. Just thinking about how the day will unfold brings a smile to your face. You can already feel the warm sun on your skin and the sweet taste of your friend's home-made peach pie.

Suddenly, your reverie is interrupted when the wind kicks up, and a steady patter of rain begins beating on the roof. You reach for your phone to check the forecast and find a stream of texts from your friends about rescheduling due to the weather. Your happy day has been called off.

How do you feel?

I know how I felt when this happened to me last summer. Initially, my reaction was one of aggravation and disappointment, even petty bitterness aimed at Mother Nature. Then I remembered that I could *think twice.* By thinking twice, I mean the two-step process of (1) paying attention to your thoughts and reactivity and noticing when you've slipped into unhelpful, even harmful, modes of thinking, and (2) redirecting those thoughts in a more positive direction. It can make all the difference, as I happily discovered once again on that overcast, drizzly morning.

Rather than drowning in negative thoughts about the weather, I paused and took a few deep breaths, then reminded myself that there was nothing I could do about the rain. What I *could* do was manage my response. *Is this really so bad?* I asked myself. *It's disappointing, for sure, but these plans will get rescheduled. At least now I get to sleep in!* In other words, thinking twice is about reconsidering your position, finding the upside in a situation, or at least adopting another perspective. When I did that, my mood eased into acceptance, then quickly morphed into appreciation and a new sense of possibility. Without a plan, suddenly there was nowhere I needed to go.

That's when I burrowed into the pillows, relishing the comfort of lingering under the covers. I shot my husband a playful text, complete with heart-winking emoji. *Perfect morning to stay in bed. Care to bring me a cup of coffee?*

A few years ago, this would have played out differently. My emotional reaction would likely have been as dismal as the weather, my disappointment lingering like a dark cloud and turning the entire day into a washout. That was before I discovered the infinite value of pausing and investigating my thoughts, of *thinking twice*.

This approach isn't new. Nor is it rocket science. But it does work, and it has been passed down through the ages, as is evident in Shakespeare's *Hamlet*: "There is nothing either good or bad, but thinking makes it so." There's also this bit of wisdom from Roman emperor Marcus Aurelius: "If you are distressed by anything external, the pain isn't due to the thing itself but to your estimate of it; and this you have the power to revoke at any moment." Or, as my father, the late great Michael Fagin always said, "Everything in life is perspective."

I used to balk at the idea of perspective, much less pausing to think twice. If my job were less stressful, if my loans were paid off, if my parents were alive, if I found love, if … if … if … *then* I would be happy. If something needed to change, it was my circumstances, not my attitude. I had goals to achieve—real, tangible goals that, once met, would add up to my best life.

But I was skipping a vital interim step. The way we think *does* have a direct and significant impact on how we feel, both physically and emotionally, as you discovered in the exercises in Chapter Two. How we feel determines how we behave. It sets the tone for how we conduct ourselves in the world, affecting everything from how we interact with others to how we move forward—or stagnate—when it comes to pursuing our goals.

For example, if I tell myself that I am unattractive and undesirable as I'm getting dressed for a party, how is my night likely to go? How will my self-criticism and insecurities impact my interactions with others? Will I be outgoing and open to meeting people, or more likely to hide away in a corner? Will I drink too much because

I need extra confidence, then miss out on truly connecting? When I leave early, feeling dejected because I didn't have any meaningful conversations (because *Who would want to talk to me?*), what will I tell myself?

When I had this conversation with a client recently, she used her "dreadful party experience" as *proof* of her unattractiveness. Her failure to connect with anyone on that night was, in her mind, solid evidence that she would always be alone. Until we explored further, her self-judgment seemed irrelevant to her. She had never considered the extent to which her attitude affected her behavior or played a role in her suffering.

Another client of mine, whom I'll call Nico, was struggling at work. He told me that his manager didn't "value" him and that he didn't feel "experienced enough" to share his opinions during team meetings. With these limiting thoughts locked and loaded, Nico couldn't possibly show up to the office with gusto and confidence. Instead, he made himself small and hid his talents, which led to others being noticed in meetings—and ultimately being promoted over him. Before learning how to think twice, Nico viewed being ignored by the manager as confirmation of disrespect, his failure to engage in the meeting as proof of his inadequacy. Making himself small only fed into the painful narrative, but with my encouragement (and lots of practice using the tools we will explore in Chapters Thirteen through Seventeen), Nico began to adjust his thinking, as did the partygoer who was full of dread. By remembering to pause and ask "why?" in these insecure moments, then thinking twice about their underlying assumptions, both were able to significantly improve their situations and self-worth.

Might you be willing to try the same? After all, even though things won't always go your way, and you have no control over the behavior of others, you *can* exert control over your thinking.

To be clear, I am not suggesting you overlook every negative thought or suddenly become a Pollyanna. Nor am I suggesting you can skip over life's difficult experiences by thinking happy thoughts. Life is undoubtedly rife with challenges, and few of them feel as manageable as a rainy day. Devastation happens, wreaking havoc and causing tremendous pain. Loss hurts, and it needs to be felt and grieved. The same is true for anger, pain, or any difficult emotion. Allowing yourself to feel your feelings is incredibly important and far more beneficial than denying them.

But when it comes to maximizing your well-being, recognizing that your thinking *also* plays a significant role in how your life unfolds is crucial. It's especially important to do this, to pause and go deeper, whenever you catch yourself thinking you suck or notice yourself caught in a familiar but unpleasant pattern of thinking and behaving. To do this, I want to teach you about a process I call the Four Cs, which stands for *clarify*, *confront*, *change*, and *continue*.

To *clarify* is to make something clearer and more comprehensible. To shed light. Clarify starts, first and always, with pausing and breathing, with getting quiet and still, focusing on the breath as you pay close attention to what you feel. What you feel may not always be pleasant, but clarifying requires you to sit with discomfort, suspend judgment, and cultivate curiosity, so the questions emerge —*Why this frustration, anger or dismay?*—as well as some answers.

To *confront* can imply argument or even battle. Confront is a bumping up against someone or something, which, in this case, is you, your thoughts, and your negative self-talk—the various ways you think you suck. But the confrontation isn't hostile. It involves learning to probe beneath the surface of your thoughts and questioning your assumptions. Together, we will explore a variety of tools to guide you through this process. And while this may not sound like your idea of a good time, as you become more aware of your beliefs, insecurities, and defenses, you'll start to see how many of your attempts to protect yourself often do more harm than good.

The next *C* is *change*. After examining and questioning your habitual self-talk, you can use the tools I will share in Chapters Thirteen through Seventeen to help you disengage from that unhelpful running dialogue. Change starts with bringing your stories to the surface and reframing them, much as I did when my plans were canceled by inclement weather. Once you do, you will feel a new confidence that allows you to shift your mindset and behavior so you can appreciate the positive things in your life that you may have previously overlooked.

Then it becomes time to simply (and sometimes not so simply) *continue* the work. To continue using the tools you'll find in these pages, to continue to clarify and confront and change.

Learning to pay attention to your thoughts is a prerequisite to greater happiness and well-being. The way you think is indeed changeable if you remind yourself to think twice—i.e., pausing after your initial negative reaction and then using the Four Cs to examine and reframe your thoughts in ways that will work to your advantage instead of dragging you down.

So rather than letting your mind roam to those dark places, let's start to learn to rein it in with some simple strategies, all of them rooted in science.

———

Exercise: Putting the Four Cs into Practice

Bring to mind a recent "rainy day" scenario of your own, such as a delayed flight, a babysitter getting sick at the last minute, or any disappointment or irritation. As you relive the scenario in your mind, notice how you feel, both physically and emotionally. Would you describe your mood as perturbed? Disconcerted? Furious? Rather than sinking into this negativity, use the Four Cs approach to clarify and confront the underlying notions that are shaping your perception. Is it the situation at hand that has you down? Might there be unhelpful thoughts in your head dictating your mood or actions? What is the story running through your mind? Perhaps it's *Nothing ever works out for me,* or *I am such an idiot.* Whatever it is, pause to *clarify* the story and name it. Then take a few more deep breaths and *confront* that negative narrative. Is it really true? Can you think of examples that show it isn't true—at least not entirely, or not all the time? Next comes *change:* Is there an alternate story you can tell? What new interpretation might help shift your perspective and possibly lead to more deliberate actions or empowered choices in the future? (That's the *continue* part.) Now how do you feel?

———

If this exercise was difficult for you, know that you will have ample opportunity to practice throughout our time together. For now, try to think of thinking twice and the Four Cs as the difference between reacting impulsively and responding with care. Once you disengage from autopilot, you can grab the wheel and take control.

FIVE

Getting to Know Your
Inner Critic Even Better

 The cave you fear to enter holds the treasure you seek.

Joseph Campbell

RECENTLY, A CLIENT ASKED ME HOW TO DIFFERENTIATE HER HARMFUL inner critiques and reactions from the kind of worries and warnings she'd *benefit* from paying attention to. Julie, a special education teacher, was in the process of building a digital platform where she could share the work she did with individual children more broadly, making her methods available to a wider audience.

She felt confident that it was a great idea but also paralyzed. "What if I really have no business putting myself out there this way?" she asked me. "Who do I think I am, declaring myself an expert and asking all of these people to pay me for a product that isn't guaranteed to deliver?"

I tried reassuring Julie that what she was attempting to do was exactly the kind of stretching, growing, and risk-taking that tends to activate our inner critics. After all, their primary concern is keeping us safe from any potential embarrassment or failure (a concept we will explore further in the next chapter).

Julie was unconvinced. "What if these fears are justified?" she persisted. "I mean, I don't have any experience working at this scale. What if it's a bust? What if I destroy my hard-earned reputation? What if I put my family's finances in jeopardy?"

Julie might as well have been speaking in the voice of her inner critic. I listened as her tone grew increasingly sarcastic, even rude, and noted her use of phrases like "have no business," "who do I think I am?" and "declaring myself an expert." Inner critics love highlighting all the ways we "aren't ready" for whatever scary endeavor we're considering. Saying we "lack the experience" or that we'll "ruin our reputation" are common inner critic techniques. (When it comes to sharing my writing, Lola tries this approach all the time.) Julie's concern about her family's financial security was also a tell since our inner critics often trade in the currency of worst-case scenarios.

In her incredible book *Playing Big: Practical Wisdom for Women Who Want to Speak Up, Create, and Lead*, Tara Mohr identifies eleven key characteristics of the inner critic, and in the interest of being thorough, here they are in their entirety:

1. Sounding harsh, rude or mean;
2. Using binary thinking (you are fabulous or horrible; you are amazing or you suck);
3. Appearing to represent your best interest by being the voice of reason;
4. Telling you, "You aren't ready yet;"
5. Doubting your skills at quantitative/negotiating/technical matters;
6. Critiquing your body or appearance;
7. Coming across like an audiotape playing on automatic, as if invading or interrupting your own thinking;
8. Repeating the same old phrases and stories over and over again (remember the lazy DJ!);
9. Sounding irrational, yet believable;
10. Resort to the "one-two punch" by first attacking you,

then shaming you for having those thoughts to begin
with (Lola always does this!); or

11. Sounding like other critical people in your life—a parent,
teacher, or boss, or even cultural or religious attitudes
you've internalized.

Clearly, Julie's ruminating and catastrophizing met many of
these! What about you? Do you recognize any of these qualities
when your inner critic speaks to you?

If so, take heart. Having a vocal inner critic does not have to be
a bad thing. It's only when we give our critic too much power,
following their lead without awareness or introspection, that we run
into problems. So, I'll suggest to you what I suggested to Julie, something I've already stressed the importance of: Just pause. (Always
pause!) Focus on your breathing. Think twice. Four C it! Seek to
clarify and confront exactly what is causing the problem. Ask yourself: Why the stress? (There's that all-important *why?* again.) Take
stock of your thoughts and emotions and ask: *What am I believing in
this moment? What am I afraid of?* The irony is, an inner critic outburst
often indicates exciting things ahead. Opportunity can be terrifying.
If you suspect your critic's presence, consider what it is they may be
trying to protect you from. Does their concern feel legitimate to you,
or is it too severe, too extreme, or even irrational?

Given that recognition and understanding are more than half
the battle, you are already on your way to less-stressful living.

Logic Games

Another tried-and-true method for recognizing your inner critic's
presence is to identify any logic games you play with yourself. For
example, do you tell yourself you need to achieve a specific title at
your organization before you feel like you've "made it," or hit a
certain number on the scale before you can feel comfortable in your
own skin? Do you believe your children must be accepted to certain
schools, or your business must hit a particular amount of revenue
before you can relax and feel good about yourself?

Inner critics love to impose these if-then logic games upon us, keeping us trapped in a restrictive, narrowly focused frame of mind. It's as if we have no right (or ability) to feel happy, confident, or proud, or even exist, until we lose twenty pounds or get married or accomplish whatever it is we are telling ourselves we must do to be successful.

Here are a few if-then stories I've heard over the years: *If only I were more of a morning person, then I would feel productive. If I were sharper and could stay focused, then my business would run so much more efficiently. If I had a few more steady clients, then I'd feel successful. If my family were more supportive, then I could achieve so much more. If my boss were more willing to delegate, then I could really show her what I am capable of! If I were smarter/more organized/wealthier/braver/in a relationship, then I could....*

These logic games are just another way we limit ourselves, undermine our self-worth, and diminish our happiness. They keep us focused on what is missing, whatever flaws we need to eradicate, or whatever it is we believe is "out there" that might finally satisfy or complete us.

What I call logic games, psychologist, author, and mindfulness expert Tara Brach calls "If-Only Mind." The first time I heard her speak on this subject, I was struggling with body insecurity myself. What began as a simple observation—that my body hadn't completely bounced back from Baby Number Three—quickly escalated to a distracting obsession. I was approaching my fitness routine with a level of intensity that I knew, deep down, was problematic, but I could not cut myself any slack.

First thing each morning, I pulled on my all-black spandex "power suit" and made a run for it, crisscrossing Central Park, rushing uptown and back down, my kids along for the ride in their tricked-out SUV-like stroller. Feel the burn, baby! And that wasn't counting the time I spent at the gym, which was every possible free moment.

The only place I let myself slow down was in front of the mirror, where I would conduct a piercing assessment of my body that was utterly devoid of appreciation, compassion, or kindness, despite the fact that it had given birth to three healthy children. With Lola's taunts in my ear, I evaluated my appearance with a laser focus on my perceived flaws—belly, arms, ass—until the parts I didn't like were all I could see. The only thing I hated more than my imperfections was the extent to which I cared about them. *You look good enough* would quickly morph into *You are shallow and ridiculous and there are far more worthy goals to pursue than washboard abs. Go play with your kids. Or better yet, go back to work!*

In other words, I was trapped in an endless cycle of self-criticism and despair, obsession and denial, and I could not seem to remove myself from that treadmill.

Hearing Brach talk about If-Only Mind shook something loose in me, allowing me to see my self-abusing pattern in a whole new way.

The question she posed was a simple one: *What if there is nothing to do and nothing to fix? What if you are exactly as you need to be?* The concept was so radical, it stopped me in my tracks. My modus operandi had always been about pursuit. Whether it was a grade or degree, a job or relationship, or the number on the scale, wasn't life all about setting goals and working to achieve them? Shouldn't we always work our hardest to be our "best" selves? Could that entire rubric really be faulty? *What if I really was fine as is?* That got me wondering about all the other logic games I had played over the years: *If I…get into this school; get married; get this job; get this raise.* When I pondered a bit, it struck me how briefly the joy of those accomplishments stayed with me. Within a day or two (or an hour), I'd return to my if-then mindset, setting some other goal that was key to my happiness. I also thought about all the losses and disappointments I believed I'd never move past, all the devastating events I couldn't possibly survive—yet I had. Then it came to me, the utter futility of if-then thinking: If there is always something to chase, then what's the point? And if reaching a long-desired goal is never all you thought it would be, what might *truly* deliver that elusive feeling of contentment?

Would I ever get to rest and relax and *just be*?

With that last question, I experienced a tremendous feeling of release. I had been believing a story: that *first* I had to perfect my body, *then* I could feel content. Intellectually, I always knew that wasn't true, that the notion was not only painful but ridiculous. But even so, it had become the drumbeat of my days, constantly playing in the background.

When will I get to rest and relax and just be? Rest. Relaxation. Permission to *just be*, imperfect parts and all. Those were my *justs*—the place of acceptance and arrival I had been craving all along, yet mistakenly believing getting "there" had something to do with my physical appearance. The moment was powerful—a visceral, full-body experience of who I could be and how I might feel without Lola's withering criticisms. The realization was enough to motivate me to start caring for myself in a whole new way.

Now it's your turn: What are your if-then stories and conditionals? Can you take a moment to consider what you *just* want?

Exercise: Logic Games

Think about and name your personal logic games, your if-then bargains with yourself. Once you've named them, pinpoint their triggers. Do these feelings arise when you compare yourself with others, look in the mirror, or sit down to pay the bills? Notice how it feels when you are consumed by if-then thinking and how you react. Ask yourself if your story is helping you in any way. Then envision how your life might look and feel different without it. Observe with compassion, and without judgment. And try to remember this: if *you* are the author of your if-then stories, that means you hold the power to rewrite them as you choose.

Lyin' Lola

My Lola is a tiny cartoon version of me, invariably clad in a badass, all-black Batgirl outfit, complete with a leather whip. She has a perpetual thought bubble over her head, one that screams, "MOVE IT!" All. The. Time. Lola has no tolerance for slacking off or anything but maximum effort. She abhors self-pity, has zero patience for whining, and can be downright mean. Even my diminutive five-foot-two stature pisses her off. In short, she is a slave driver with a major Napoleon complex.

Now I'd like to invite you to get a little playful with the scaredy-cat scratching up *your* head.

Much as it might seem like a form of torture, I encourage all my clients to describe and sketch out their own inner critics in detail, creating an actual character as I did with Lola. Though she loomed large throughout my life, I never gave Lola a name or a persona until I read the life-changing, must-read book, *Reform Your Inner Mean Girl: 7 Steps to Stop Bullying Yourself and Start Loving Yourself*, by Amy Ahlers and Christine Arylo. I find the exercise adds a little levity and much-needed separation from our inner critic, helping us to step back, stop taking ourselves so seriously, and even have a good laugh at our own expense. Most important, it can provide a framework that helps shed light on deeply held insecurities and self-imposed limitations, while allowing a little distance from those painful beliefs.

One of my clients, Jake, calls his inner critic The Joker. He even bought Batman, Robin, and Joker action figures—his idea, which I've since encouraged many others to copy—and keeps them on a shelf by his desk. Every time Jake feels himself slipping into the weighty, "moving through sludge" feeling that signals The Joker's presence, he grabs his toys and stages a little battle, complete with sound effects, just like he did as a little boy. Batman and Robin always win, of course, and The Joker sulks back to his place on the shelf, defeated and dismissed for the day. All of this takes less than a minute, but it allows Jake to laugh at himself. Better still, it disrupts the old pattern in which Jake would feel triggered, lose confidence and allow The Joker to derail his day. Now, by playfully confronting his inner critic, Jake effectively stops The Joker in his tracks, then returns to whatever he was doing with more peace of mind.

I've had clients name their inner critics after neighborhood kids who used to pick on them or make them feel bad about themselves. Others have gone with bossy titles like The Judge, The Dictator, and The Taskmaster, just to name a few. Some have come up with more colorful names I don't want my kids to read.

Whatever you conjure up, the idea is to externalize your inner critic or, as Tara Mohr puts it, to learn "how to let the inner critic do its thing, without taking direction from it."[6] Separating "the critic" from "you" makes it easier to defuse the charge of all that negativity, as does turning it into something diminutive or comical. Once you shift the old power dynamic, you're likely to realize your critic is not so intimidating after all; in fact, it's even something of a buffoon, an overblown know-it-all. Realizing this will help you put it in its place, undermining its power and reminding you that your critic is not in charge. You are.

———

Exercise: Characterize Your Critic

Give your inner critic a name, appearance, and identity, then get creative and have fun with it by filling in the details: What music does she listen to? What are her favorite foods? What is her personal style? Does she remind you of anyone you know, real or fictional? Sketch her out in all of her glory, including whatever characteristics feel meaningful to you. As a bonus, find an object or image to represent your critic, whether an action figure, magazine photo, or a drawing of your own.

———

Your inner critic, of course, doesn't really have an independent existence; she is a function of your mind. Giving her a separate identity, however, allows you to loosen her hold. That's what I mean when I say it creates separation, making it easier to remember that she does not define you.

When you overidentify with your critic, it's easy to lose sight of that. In contrast, carefully paying attention to what she says—as well as when, where, why, and how she says it—can help you engage meaningfully and productively with your fears, rather than letting them control you. Telling ourselves we suck is part of our survival instinct. The problem is, when we comply, we limit ourselves. We may stay safe, but we also miss out.

SIX

A Smidgen of Science

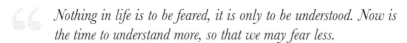 *Nothing in life is to be feared, it is only to be understood. Now is the time to understand more, so that we may fear less.*

Marie Curie

NOW THAT YOU'VE SPENT SOME TIME GETTING BETTER ACQUAINTED with your inner critic, I'd like to assure you that your negative instincts are fairly easy to retrain. You are not an old dog, and you can learn new tricks. Shifts *do* happen. People *can* change. With patience and perseverance, it's entirely possible to alter unhelpful patterns and move in a more positive direction.

Personally, I believe that it's far easier to do this when you understand a little bit about brain science—something I always talk about with my clients. Lola would prefer I go earn a doctorate in neuroscience, or at least psychology, before I share this information with you, but I have politely declined her request. Instead, I will do my best to explain some incredibly complex concepts in very broad strokes. I'll start with the survival instinct and the negativity bias, both of which can make it difficult to change our ways. I'll also talk about neuroplasticity, which refers to the fact that the brain itself can change, causing us to change. I'm focusing on these three ideas because they have played an important role in my personal transformation from a cynical and dismissive lawyer to a more open and accepting life coach. More importantly, this science explains why we are so hard on ourselves and gives added motivation for taking better care of our body and brain so we can feel and live better.

Before we dive in, here's a story about Victoria, a woman I met at an airport bar at LAX. I was wrapping up a whirlwind week filled with work, travel, socializing, and networking, and though I'd enjoyed it, I was exhausted. With only a few hours before my red-eye home, I was sipping a glass of Sancerre and thoroughly enjoying my first moments of solitude in days. Next thing I knew, a woman in a chic black suit plopped down beside me. What I remember most clearly is how instantly my defenses reared up, as if her presence in this very public place was some form of personal affront. *What? Noooooo! This place is practically empty! Why sit right next to me?*

None too subtly, I sized her up. Crisp, white button-down; expensive purse; straight, shiny blonde hair that looked professionally blown dry. Within seconds, I cast her in the role of a cold, harried, judgmental corporate type, self-important in her stress, pressed for time, and definitely dismissing me—in my ripped jeans, leather jacket, and unruly curls—as an insignificant nobody. That is, if she even bothered to notice me at all. Besides that, she reeked of tension, her negativity palpable. The last thing I wanted to do was engage. I practically turned away from her on my barstool.

Looking back, it is so clear and embarrassing how much my snap judgment revealed about my own insecurities at that time. Had the bartender not just brought my salad, I might have gotten up to leave. Instead, in an effort to further shield myself from Victoria and her bad energy, I reached into my bag to grab my headphones, planning to retreat into my audiobook.

But something else happened instead. Without giving it any conscious thought and surprising myself just as much as Victoria, I turned toward her and placed my hand gently on her upper arm.

"Excuse me," I ventured.

Victoria looked at me, eyes wide with surprise.

"Are you okay?" I asked before I could stop myself.

Immediately, her surprised eyes began to well up with tears.

"Why are you asking me that?" she managed, without a hint of defensiveness or hostility in her voice. There was only vulnerability and a stunned sense of gratitude at being seen.

"I don't know," I answered honestly. "You seem … troubled. *Are* you okay?"

At that, her tears flowed freely, as did her story. She was, in fact, harried and stressed and entirely overwhelmed, but this had nothing to do with her career or any feelings of self-importance. Her father was dying, and Victoria felt wrecked and desperate at the thought of losing him.

I forgot about the headphones and the salad and spent the next hour listening as Victoria shared the details of her father's condition, as well as some added stressors due to prickly family dynamics. I briefly mentioned my own experience with loss, but mostly, I listened before leaving her with a hug and a quick exchange of contact information. As I settled into my seat on the plane, I took a last look at my phone. There was a text from Victoria already, thanking me for my compassion and thanking the universe for putting me in her path. That was almost ten years ago. Victoria and I have remained in touch to this day.

Wired to Survive

Strange as it may seem, this story has everything to do with brain science. My initial reaction to Victoria was defensive, visceral, and self-protective. This is a classic fear response. Fear is an essential component of staying alive. Our bodies are designed to react quickly and instinctively to threats, and we do so without much rational thought. This built-in protection system is known as the fight-or-flight response (or the fight-flight-freeze response, or the acute stress response). It is a physiological reaction that happens when we sense danger of any kind, and it starts in the brain and spills through the body. For example, you hear a loud bang and instinctively duck for cover, crouching in a protective position and covering your head before you've even registered what is happening. Or you spy a bear up ahead on a hiking trail and stop immediately in your tracks, even before you know it *is* a bear (which may not be common where you live but happens near my house all the time!).

When you perceive some threat—real or psychological—your nervous system responds by releasing neurochemicals and hormones that, in turn, trigger a series of physiological responses, including increased heart rate, blood pressure, and respiration. You might get pale or flushed, or cold and clammy. Your extremities can become numb or tingly and your pupils might dilate.

These physical responses are meant to help you survive a threatening situation and can be extremely beneficial when you are in actual danger. But all too often, there is no real danger. (Exhibit A: my instinctive alarm when Victoria sat beside me.)

Yet our brains see danger everywhere, constantly launching us into reactivity. It's a "better safe than sorry" impulse that, sadly, often backfires. You snap at your mother for commenting on your haircut because you feel judged, and bickering ensues (fight). You avoid following up with a potential new client because you don't want to seem pushy or overeager (flight). Your mind goes blank when you are asked an unexpected question in the middle of a presentation, because you're afraid you'll look unprepared, foolish, or unprofessional (freeze). You get aggressive or meek, you decline challenges or procrastinate on projects because you are thinking insecure "I suck" thoughts (fight, flight, freeze!).

In short, it's tough to think straight when we are in a heightened and triggered state. Our prefrontal cortex—the most evolved part of the human brain and the seat of rational thought and clear decision-making—goes mostly offline, while the brain stem and limbic system, the more primitive parts of the brain linked to instinct and emotion, take over. Clear thinking is impaired, as are higher-order functions such as planning, reasoning, risk assessment, problem-solving, empathy, and emotional control. Productive, rational responses —organizing, sorting, self-control, connecting, prioritizing, and focusing—are less available.[7]

But there is a way to interrupt this process. If you pause, even briefly, you'll give the rest of the brain—the logical part of the brain that goes offline whenever we are triggered—a chance to flip back on. Better still, when you begin to breathe deeply and intentionally, you'll activate the parasympathetic nervous system and allow the body to calm down so more helpful and productive instincts can come into play. That's when you remember that your mom is lovable and dependable, whether she approves of your hair or not. You can summon the courage to follow up on potential business, reminding yourself you have nothing to lose and everything to gain. You recall that whether you know the answer to every question or not, you can do your best to offer some form of response, even if it's "Can I research that and get back to you later?"

Phew.

———

Exercise: Your Fear Response

To conjure up your fear response, try to recall an unpleasant moment with another person, whether a friend or stranger, that made you feel scared, angry, or upset. Perhaps it was someone who cut you off in traffic or was otherwise driving irresponsibly. Perhaps someone snapped at you unexpectedly or overreacted to something you did. Maybe it was a friend or family member who made a careless comment or hurt your feelings in some way. Whatever it was, recall the scenario and relive the experience for a moment. Think about where you were, what you were doing, and how you felt just before the encounter. Then recall what triggered you. What exactly did the person do or say? What were the thoughts circling through your mind? How long did it take for you to become upset, scared, or angry? What did you experience, physically, throughout your body? What was the story you told yourself about this other person, and what judgments did you form?

Whatever your personal fear response looks like, know this: You can tame it by pausing and breathing, returning yourself to a calmer state. Simply inhaling and exhaling, deeply and deliberately, as you focus on the sensation of breathing, is all it takes. If appropriate, remind yourself that you are safe and secure, as well as capable of handling the situation. Proceed from this steadier, less triggered place, grateful for the knowledge that such a simple tool—pausing and breathing—wields such tremendous power.

―――――

The Negativity Bias

For our ancestors, the ability to scan the environment for danger was crucial. Those who were vigilant and alert, keeping their attention laser-focused on dangerous predators and potential threats, were far more likely to stay alive than those wandering blithely through the fields, searching for flowers and gazing with wonder at the beautiful scenery. Our brains developed accordingly.

This aspect of our survival instinct is known as negativity bias, and it's why we are far more attuned to the bad stuff around us than the good—and why our negative experiences tend to have a greater psychological impact on us than our positive experiences.

Blame negativity bias when you find yourself focusing on the small bit of critical feedback you received in a mostly positive performance review. Or when you harp on a minor misstep by your spouse while overlooking everything he does right. When you stare at the ceiling on sleepless nights, rehashing mistakes you've made; when you can't stop thinking about all the ways you or your life could or should be better; or when your daily thoughts are largely consumed by tasks to tackle or issues to resolve, you can thank your negativity bias for that too.

Painful, right?

Negativity bias may have played a key role in evolution, keeping our ancestors safe and ensuring human survival, but it can hurt us in modern life. Not only does it make us unhappy—repeatedly drawing our attention to problems instead of everything we have to appreciate—but it can make us excessively hard on ourselves and others. It can also hold us back from accomplishing our goals and extending ourselves toward others. Take my initial reaction to Victoria: something about her presence triggered Lola and activated my fight-flight-freeze response before she even uttered a word. We humans are sensitive creatures! We pick up on the sadness, anger, and fear emanating from others. The negative energy radiating from Victoria that day had nothing to do with me, but it registered in my body as an attack. Meanwhile, my reaction had nothing to do with the actual Victoria. It was my perception of her that triggered my defensiveness, launching me into counterattack. I imagined her to be judging me, so I got judgmental, too, creating an overall negative feedback loop that made me want to move away and reach for my headphones.

And to think that all Victoria was doing was sitting there minding her own business, feeling sad about her father. If this kind of thing didn't happen between people all the time, it might actually be funny. *A woman walks into a bar...*

As Daniel Goleman writes in his groundbreaking book *Emotional Intelligence: Why It Can Matter More Than IQ*, "We transmit and catch moods from each other in what amounts to a subterranean economy of the psyche in which some encounters are toxic, some nourishing."[8] Fortunately, a nourishing instinct saved me that day. Extending that hand, then expressing concern, filled me with warmth and worth, allowing Victoria to soften too. One minute she held her grief like a shield, unwittingly scaring away anyone who might be willing to help. I was protecting myself in much the same way, far too quick to judge Victoria before she had a chance to judge me.

This, unfortunately, happens between people far too often, whether with strangers sharing the briefest encounters, or colleagues and friends—or even the people we love most. We miscommunicate and make assumptions. We react to the words and actions of others through the filter of our own fears, insecurities, and perceptions.

Our lying, insecure minds twist the facts, making us wary and mistrusting, judgmental, defensive, and occasionally hostile.

My encounter with Victoria helped me embrace a better way, and that is the lesson I hope to convey. It *is* possible to override primitive instincts and interact from a more evolved position. We *can* make it a habit to pause and breathe before reacting, to check in with ourselves and question our assumptions. We *can* consider how our thinking might be coloring any tense situation, then aim to proceed from a calmer, less triggered state. At the very least, we can learn to stay present and curious, to confront ourselves before confronting others.

In the past, I'd always come down hard on myself for my reactivity and the narrow-minded judgments I couldn't quite shake. I wanted to be kinder and gentler—with myself and others—but often found myself slipping back to a less forgiving place. I wanted to be more appreciative of the many blessings of my life but couldn't quite help obsessing over problems and deficiencies. I felt so much better once I understood that it was all rooted in evolutionary biology and the instinct to survive.

Translation: it wasn't my fault. And it's not yours either.

We are hardwired to do this, to keep ourselves alive. At the same time, we are not destined to wallow in negativity, nor are we powerless against the painful patterns caused by our doubts and insecurities. We have the ability to learn and change—to overcome our self-critical or fear-based instincts and rewire our brains for greater positivity. That's thanks to something called neuroplasticity.

Neuroplasticity

Until recently, scientists believed that the human brain hardly changed after childhood, and that by the time we reached adulthood, our brains were mostly fixed. Now, after decades of scientific research and study, we know the human brain is adaptable and malleable throughout the course of our lifetime, reorganizing itself whenever we learn new things and have new experiences—a phenomenon known as neuroplasticity.

Neural pathways form and deepen every time we think, feel, or take action. Some neural pathways are incredibly well traveled, like the ruts on a dirt driveway through which the owner drives again and again. Through repetition, tire tracks form and then deepen. The driver, though capable of steering the car out of the tracks and creating new ones, rarely does. Sticking with the well-worn path is much easier.

The same is true of our habits, our established ways of thinking and behaving. This isn't necessarily a bad thing. Habits can be amazing shortcuts—they are why most of us don't think twice about brushing our teeth each morning. By the same token, each time we think the same negative thoughts (*I'm a loser*) or perform the same activity (bite our fingernails), that pathway deepens and becomes more instinctive.

With intention and effort, however, all of us are capable of blazing new neural paths. Each time we interrupt our habitual patterns of thinking and doing and steer ourselves in a new direction—each time we switch up our thoughts and behaviors—we begin to carve a new groove into the structure of our brain. Over time, the more we travel the new path, the more instinctive it becomes.

I think of negativity bias and neuroplasticity as the one-two punch of radical transformation. We *can* rewire our brains away from "I suck" negativity—or any other unhelpful thought or habit—by learning to recognize and interrupt those patterns, then redirecting ourselves to a happier, more confident and evolved state.

SEVEN

The Power of Pausing

 Human freedom involves our capacity to pause between the stimulus and response and, in that pause, to choose the one response toward which we wish to throw our weight.

Rollo May

INSTINCTS ARE NOT DESTINY. NEITHER ARE HABITS. WHATEVER THE decision at hand—whether to turn left or right, to eat a salad or a burger, to fire off an angry email or save it for a calmer moment— you can *choose* your course of action. The same is true for heeding or ignoring the chatter in your head.

Think back to the exercises you did in Chapter Two. How many times throughout your life has your negativity playlist run through your mind, whether subtly or overtly? Has it ever occurred to you to question the truth of those insults, or draw any connections between them and your way of being in the world? And what about the next time your inner critic starts singing its favorite tunes—what will you do? Will you abide by the abuse, buying into those same old tired stories and continuing along the same old sorry path? Or will you choose something else, forging new neural pathways and new ways of being?

Your ability to choose effectively begins, as always, with pausing.

Pausing sounds so simple, and it is. But it is also impactful. In fact, *just pause and breathe* is always the advice I give when anyone asks me for one easy tool for improving daily life.

Remember, when you pause and breathe, taking deep, slow, purposeful breaths, you calm your nervous system and deactivate your fight-flight-freeze response. This approach reduces stress and increases focus. It helps you get centered, grounded, and clear-headed, and it ultimately leads to better decision-making in difficult moments. Just as important, pausing is the gateway to awareness, the most essential component in making positive change. After all, you won't correct a behavior you don't notice, can't solve a problem you don't recognize or comprehend. It makes sense, doesn't it? If you are going to free yourself from the pain and heaviness of your "I suck" thoughts, you are going to need to notice them first.

Yet most of us live with little to no appreciation of what's *actually* troubling or driving us moment to moment. I marched to the beat of Lola's drum for years before I developed any conscious awareness of her existence. In those earlier go-go-go years, I had no patience for slowing down or pausing. I had places to go and things to accomplish! I took tremendous pride in how much I was getting done, never mind that my experiences felt rushed, harried, and rather empty. My always-on, always-be-productive way of life was entirely addictive—and on autopilot.

In fact, when I think back on that period, I like to compare it to spending time in a casino, a place deliberately made to block out awareness. There is a reason there are no hard stops, right angles, clocks, or windows in a casino. The odds, after all, are always in the house's favor. They want you to stay at the table, focused only on your game of choice. The longer, the better. Every impetus you might have to pause, look around, consider the time, or register your surroundings is discouraged by design. Casinos are all about reducing friction—or, rather, *preventing oppor-tunities for people to pause*, even for a moment. If you don't pause, you are less likely to question your behavior or opt for something different.

So much of modern life, from the constant barrage of outrageous headlines to the hypnotic pull of our devices, functions this way. It's so easy to get caught up in it all and end up in a trancelike state, which makes it difficult to notice what is happening, question how you are feeling, or think about what you might choose to do differently. It becomes a habit, moving in that mindless state, rarely stepping back to question what we are doing, why we are doing it, or how it all feels. With just the slightest bit of awareness, however, it's possible to disrupt this pattern.

Consider this your cordial invitation to notice how often you operate in an unaware state. Then try doing the opposite.

It was a hard realization for me to acknowledge. Throughout my early years of motherhood, crossing items off my to-do list—shuttling the kids around town, scheduling appointments, making dinner —often carried the same sense of urgency for me as my law firm assignments once did, even as one day blurred into the next. I was so preoccupied with doing and accomplishing—still buying into Lola's old story that my worth was tied to how hard I worked—that I never bothered to stop and notice what was happening, let alone how it was making me feel or the lack of necessity for all that self-imposed pressure. Instead, I rushed from place to place, priding myself on my "productivity." But I'd forgotten why I'd left lawyering in the first place: to *be* with my children, to mother them meaningfully and fully experience their childhoods, not to *manage* them most efficiently. Meanwhile, my best memories always seemed to come from the more spontaneous, slower moments—the rainy days we decided to have an impromptu baking session or when we'd detour from an errand to take an unhurried stroll through Central Park.

And then came the garbage can races.

I was only a year into life coaching, and my children were very young. We had recently moved to Connecticut, and I was still getting used to our new routines. Rob was staying in the city a few nights a week, and I was doing my best to balance a new career with full-time motherhood. This meant working and studying as much as possible during the kids' school hours, as well as cooking, cleaning, grocery shopping, and endless driving. Tuesdays were especially challenging, involving a complicated combination of piano lessons and soccer practice. This required nearly three hours behind the wheel, crossing back and forth (and back and forth) across rugged backroads to get everyone dropped off, picked up, and where they needed to be at the appropriate time. And then everyone needed dinner.

I remember one Tuesday, driving home, the trunk loaded with groceries, the kids chatty and slaphappy in the backseat, my mind roaming everywhere but the present moment. Mostly, I was preoccupied by all that I still had to do, lost in a mental movie of the night to come: Get home. Park and unload the car. Preheat oven. Put away groceries. Marinate chicken. Slice and dice vegetables. Orchestrate showers, oversee homework, set the table, etc.… Underneath all of those to-dos was Lola, filling me with self-doubt and shame: *Maybe we shouldn't have moved to Connecticut. Why didn't you organize all of this earlier today? Maybe you shouldn't have gone back to work. Why don't you accept your role as "Mommy"—it's not a bad life—and stop trying to have it all? Are you really this bent out of shape over dinner and bedtime? What has happened to you?* Looking back, I was exhausted and slightly overwhelmed. I was stuck in that sticky web of beliefs where I had to be firing on all cylinders, doing everything perfectly, but unwilling to accept my limitations—or the realities of time.

But then I remembered to pause and breathe.

That was how I caught it, that old swirl. I noticed my hunched shoulders and crinkled brow and the tightness of my hands gripping the wheel. My children's laughter, there along but mostly drowned out by the chatter in my head, suddenly broke through. I took a beat and looked in the rearview mirror, taking in the sight of them. They were adorable, side by side in their booster seats, sippy cups and snack bags in hand, blabbing about their days. *They weren't worrying about the night ahead, let alone rating me according to how much I had/hadn't accomplished all day, so why should I?* I turned into the driveway and noticed the garbage cans sitting there from early in the morning. *Ugh*, I remember thinking initially, *one more thing to do.*

But as we pulled into the garage, I paused again, hoping to recapture that wider, more forgiving perspective from a moment ago. The groceries could wait. So could showers and homework and all the rest. It was true, there was still a lot to do, but nobody was watching, assessing, or caring how it all got done. And my intense approach was only making me feel worse. *Why not let life be fun instead?*

"Who wants to race me to the garbage cans?" I sang out.

All three kids clamored out of the car and went tearing down the driveway, squealing and laughing and crashing into one another. I never even joined the race, but stood there, watching them, enjoying the moment and recording it in my mind. I can still see the evening sky, easing its way from bright blue to soft, rosy pink, the perfect background for the autumn trees, resplendent in every shade of red, orange, and bright yellow. I can still smell the hint of apples and freshly mown grass in the air, still hear the sounds of tiny sneakers spraying gravel as they ran. And I can still feel the relief and pleasure that came from stepping out of my stress to relax and savor the experience of watching my children drag those trash cans across the driveway.

It was a perfect moment—one that I came very close to missing while lost in the planning, ruminating, and "shoulding" in my mind.

How many moments are you sacrificing, and how might you implement a simple pause- and-breathe approach to get them back?

Learning to integrate this technique into my own life has been one of the greatest gifts I've given myself and one I hope to give you as well. It is a small but significant shift in behavior that yields tremendous results, and it is an essential first step on the way to positive transformation.

It won't always be easy. As simple as it may be to pause and breathe, stopping to make deliberate choices—as opposed to operating on autopilot—requires effort. And most of us do not like to overexert ourselves! In fact, the human brain is a masterful machine designed for maximum efficiency with minimal effort. That's another reason we often default to routine habits, both mental and physical, whether they work to our advantage or not.

Think about those self-critical, self-effacing thoughts again. How habitual are they? How frequently have the same themes and phrases spun through your mind or dictated your behavior? And how often have you stopped to notice what was happening, let alone redirect yourself? Now think about activities like showering, flipping on the coffee machine, or commuting to work. We tend to do these the same way every day without thinking much about them. Both are examples of automatic behaviors, habits born of repetition. In the case of cementing desirable habits, this human tendency toward patterning and repetition is a beautiful thing. I used to have to force myself to exercise, summoning the motivation and overcoming all manner of excuses each time. Now it is *just something I do.* Every morning, instead of hitting the snooze button (my old habit), I put on my exercise clothes (laying them out the night before helps), roll out my yoga mat, and begin my routine. I don't have to make special plans or expend any effort to motivate myself. I no longer even think about it. Instead, after years of repeating the behavior, it's as much a habit as brushing my teeth or making my bed.

But for unhealthy, unwanted, or destructive habits—in my case, reaching for my phone during any down moment, prioritizing work while neglecting my household, or beating myself up in my mind— the automatic habit thing can do us a disservice.

Pausing helps me pay closer attention, which makes it easier to name and deconstruct any automatic behaviors or thoughts that detract from my life and replace them with more deliberate actions and reflections. This is one of the countless reasons I recommend meditation to almost all of my clients, and I'd be remiss not to mention it here. Because meditation promotes greater awareness, and adopting a regular practice can help you establish a new instinct in the face of challenge: to pause and breathe and get curious before reacting. And the benefits of that? Spending even just a few moments focusing on your breathing can activate your parasympathetic nervous system—the body's built-in mechanism for unwinding the stress response and slowing and calming the mind. This can defuse tension and limit reactivity, and in the process, lead to more thoughtful and intentional behavior.

I'd like you to pause here and check in with yourself. Notice how you feel, starting with physical sensations: Are you too warm or cold? Are you comfortable or would you like to switch your position? How is your energy level? Are you hungry? How would you describe your emotional state? At this point, I am not suggesting you make any changes. I am simply asking you to practice pausing, breathing, and noticing.

Next, if you're willing, I'd like to suggest a lengthier exercise, described below. This one is intended to help you experience the power of pausing for yourself and, hopefully, incorporate it as a new habit.

––––––

Exercise: Let's Play POQR

This exercise helps you establish a new habit, one that will clarify what truly makes you content and what drags you down. Begin by setting three different alarms on your phone at three different times of day, ideally timed for when you will be doing different activities. Label the alarm "POQR" (pronounced "poker") which stands for *pause, observe, question, reflect*. Each time you're alerted, I want you to: (1) *pause* what you are doing; (2) *observe* what you are feeling (both your specific physical sensations and any emotions that have arisen); (3) *question* why you might be feeling that way— whether it is a function of your current activity or something circling through your mind; and then (4) *reflect*. Is the experience familiar or unusual? Positive or negative? Try not to judge or analyze; simply notice.

Next, grab a notebook and record your observations. As you continue to use POQR, you'll want to think more about your life at large and connecting the dots. Which situations lend themselves to more positive states, and which trigger more negative feelings?

Later, we will look at tools to help you put this information to use and disrupt your unhelpful patterns. At this stage, you are simply training yourself to pause, become present, observe yourself, and draw new insights. The idea is to make pausing more instinctual and to help you become more mindful of the attitudes, ideas, and feelings that can be so easy to ignore, suppress, or miss.

———

In our first session together, one of my clients, Jill, told me how, over the years, she had come to believe that making other people happy was not just her job, but her "superpower." A mom, wife, eldest daughter, and educator, Jill was proud of her devotion to others. It was such an integral part of her identity that silencing her own needs to do for everyone else had become second nature, so much so that she didn't always realize she was doing it. By the time we met, she barely knew what *she* wanted anymore—only that she wanted things to change.

I encouraged her to try playing POQR for two weeks, and she found it revelatory. Almost immediately, she noticed how often she felt tense, overwhelmed, and resentful about how she spent her time, silently blaming her husband and sons for burdening her even as she was the one obeying all those "shoulds" and "have-tos" in her mind. Whether it was skipping the gym to go grocery shopping, caring for their new rescue puppy, or folding laundry, Jill started to see how often she assumed the onus of every household task, while neglecting more personal priorities like exercising or seeing friends. Yet she had never paused to observe her pattern, let alone question why she was doing it or how it made her feel. Nor had she ever reflected upon who was really to blame. The more she thought about it, the more it dawned on her that she had never even *asked* anyone in her family to help—hadn't even given them a chance to come to her assistance.

Jill's story is a common one, especially among my women clients, who, broadly speaking, have been brought up to believe that they "should" be caring and nurturing to a fault. Cultural norms are powerful, and all too easy to internalize. It's no wonder that for so many women, our sense of self-worth has a way of getting tied to how much we do for others. Jill was already somewhat aware of this, which is why she sought me out, but her first week with POQR painted a much fuller picture of the toll her habit was taking.

I had a similarly powerful experience when I first began paying attention to how I felt in my body throughout the day. By deliberately making the connection between my various thoughts and activities and the way I was feeling, I came to recognize a sad little pattern I had been perpetuating without even knowing it.

At the end of each day, just as my husband was coming home from work, I had been unwittingly and habitually flipping my internal switch from playful and lighthearted to deflated and serious. I was doing this all by myself but very much blaming Rob. On more than one occasion, I accused him of being the "dark cloud" in our family, too consumed by stress at work and dragging the rest of us down with him.

POQR helped me see how unfair I was being.

It was true that Rob was going through a stressful period at work and often came home a bit drained. My reaction to that, however, had everything to do with the fact that I still hadn't made peace with my status as an ex-lawyer. Intellectually, I knew the job of raising my children was incredibly important. But my deeper belief—a "Do More, Be More" story I was totally unaware of at the time—had me in a punishing stranglehold. According to that story, staying home to raise my children rendered me inferior, even childish, especially compared with my husband, who was still out there in the "real world," earning our keep and "being a grown-up." I was working hard, too, of course, but by comparison, that work didn't seem challenging or serious or even that stressful (at least compared with law firm life!). Without realizing it, I was equating stress with seriousness and struggle with validity. By that logic, I instinctively felt I needed to "match" my husband's after-work mood. So rather than continuing the dance parties and other silliness I had going on with the kids during the day and hoping he might join in, I felt I needed to appear just as harried and frustrated as he did. Then I turned around and blamed him for darkening my light.

As author, nun, and Buddhist teacher Pema Chodron writes, "Let difficulty transform you, and it will."

Through POQR, I was able to recognize the pattern and then summon the curiosity to ask the right questions. What was the story I was telling myself that was causing me to tense up at the end of each day? What were the thoughts I was believing about Rob, or about myself, that were making me resentful and angry? I came to understand that it all went back to my familiar belief that my value was tied to work—demanding, intellectually challenging, strenuous work. Through this lens, being silly and having fun with my children rendered me a lightweight, even spoiled and frivolous.

It took pausing, observing, questioning, and reflecting to help me understand the pattern. Once I did so, I was able to devise a strategy to disrupt it, and the entire family was better off for it. It started with pausing (I can't say it enough) and observing my mood, physical sensations, and behavior, and then asking the right questions, patiently exploring the ideas that were causing me pain, and laying them to rest. Was it true that taking a break from the law to raise my children made me a "lightweight"? Did it mean that I was any less intelligent or hardworking? Did it mean that I sucked?

As for my devoted and supportive husband, I stopped viewing him as a "dark cloud" whose mood I had to match and gave up blaming him for bringing us all down. Instead, I tried a new approach. When I heard him walk through the door, we all kept up with the fun and dancing. The change in our family dynamic was practically instantaneous. Suddenly Rob was matching *our* mood, leaving the stress of the day behind and joining in on the fun.

EIGHT

Consider Your Many Selves

 Do any of us understand ourselves? All the different selves that each of us is?

Mary Louisa Molesworth

I WANT TO SHARE A FAVORITE STORY THAT HAS ALWAYS RESONATED with me. I first heard it from Tara Brach, whom I mentioned earlier and whose talks are full of wit, wisdom, comfort, and inspiration. She shared a tale that took place sometime in the past in Southeast Asia, where there was an enormous plaster and clay statue of the Buddha. It was not a particularly beautiful statue, but the towns-people highly cherished it. After a long drought, a crack appeared in the statue, and some local monks came to investigate. Using tiny flashlights, they peeked through the crack and saw what appeared to be a flash of gold. After that, they started shining light into every crack they could, and each time, they saw the same flickers of gold. Eventually, they dismantled the plaster and clay, which turned out to be nothing more than a protective cover for the largest solid gold statue of the Buddha in Southeast Asia.

I'll admit I don't know how accurate this story is, but I don't think it much matters. What I love are the visuals and the symbolism. I can picture the original monks, determined to protect their precious golden Buddha from harm, dutifully layering it up with its rougher, uglier plaster exterior, durable but unremarkable in every way. Meanwhile, that casting hides something solid and pure, extraordinary and beautiful. Over time, the statue and its covering became one and the same. The essential nature—the gold—had been concealed for so long that it was forgotten. The protective coating was all anyone could see.

Aren't all of us walking around with a protective coating that covers our essence because we believe we must just to make it in this rough-and-tumble world? Life knocks us around, and we learn to toughen up along the way. Not to mention that we all need to conform, at least a little bit, to function in society. And so we learn to play by the rules—to wait our turn, second-guess our feelings and instincts, and be agreeable to fit in. We internalize values about what it takes to be worthy and successful: achievement, hard work, cooperation, commitment, compromise, and all the rest. But is it possible that we've all gone a bit too far? Could it be that you're hiding your gold, covered over by so many layers of protection that you're not quite sure who you are or what you really want anymore? And might it be possible to let yourself be as shiny and valuable as you truly are at your core? Couldn't you benefit from remembering your gold and reconnecting with your essence?

Bringing Yourself Into Harmony

We all live with multiple selves—the ones we show the world and the ones deep inside us, sometimes so deep we don't even know they are there. According to a model of psychotherapy known as Internal Family Systems (IFS), we are all made up of multiple parts, or "subpersonalities," each with their own qualities and roles to play, based on their unique memories and purpose. Beneath these multiple subpersonalities lies a "core" or "true" self, the proverbial golden Buddha stripped of its covering. We Martha Beck coaches refer to these two layers—subpersonalities and core personality—as our "social" and "essential" selves, a concept I first came across in Beck's 2001 book, *Finding Your Own North Star: Claiming the Life You Were Meant to Live.*

The social self is largely shaped by family, friends, and the culture we live in. It's concerned with following the rules, fitting in, and being liked, as well as position and status, safety and advancement. It is not inherently "bad," but it tends to be guided by the expectations and values of other people. Your social self is what gets you up with your alarm when you'd rather sleep in. It keeps you glued to your desk working when you have a deadline; it may also pressure you to stay focused on appearances and pleasing others rather than honoring your own comfort or needs. To some degree, a functioning and civil society depends on our honoring these conventions, but you can also blame your social self for much of that exhausting dialogue in your head. And like its close cousin, the inner critic, our social self lives according to a set of unwritten laws we may barely be aware of following but wouldn't dream of shirking, so rigidly does it adhere to the internalized values and notions of those around us. Count on your social self to constantly remind you of all the things you "should" and "shouldn't" be doing, all the commitments you "have to" honor or the deep desires you simply "can't" pursue.

By contrast, your essential self is like a young child who hasn't yet learned all the rules of engagement and lives with abandon; it's the driving force behind yearning, longing, seeking, hoping, and dreaming. The essential self is less practical and fearful and more passionate. It's more heart than head, more instinct than analysis. It is confident and self-assured, fiercely loving but also comfortable in solitude. Our essential selves are less self-conscious, freer from doubts, expectations, or limitations. I think of the essential self as the core of your being (i.e., the golden Buddha); in other words, the essence of who you are and what you *just* want.

Where your social self is concerned with safety and position, your essential self is gunning for you to live your best possible life. Your social self wants you to fit in while your essential self wants you to feel fully alive. We absolutely need them both, but we suffer whenever we deny one and overidentify with the other. The trick is to learn how to keep the two in balance, which isn't always easy to do.

When I was younger, I believed I was the only one living with the constant confusion and uncertainty caused by my multiple selves. Back then, I referred to them as the "warring factions of my personality," a phenomenon I always attributed to my entirely opposite but equally influential parents. For years, I pictured each persona perched on either shoulder like an angel/devil cartoon, one prompting me to keep striving for greatness—or at least constant improvement—and never resting on my laurels, while the other urged me to be more accepting and unconditionally loving toward myself. The internal tug-of-war often left me disheartened and despairing, destined to remain stuck in place or dissatisfied no matter which way I turned. Then I read Beck's *Finding Your Own North Star* and began to feel some relief. The book provided new context for my inner turmoil—I was not the only one!—and a framework for me to begin to acknowledge, appreciate, and respect each of my personas, which turned out to be the best way to bring them into harmony.

Now I'd like to ask you to do the same.

––––––

Exercise: Meet Your Multiple Selves

In the interest of getting to know your "selves" better, I'd like you to grab your notebook and answer a few questions:

- Can you think of any situations where you edit yourself or modify your behavior to be nice, respectful, polite, appropriate, or accepted? How often and when and where do you feel this way?
- How often do you conduct yourself according to what

you "should" or "have to" do, or what you "shouldn't"
or "mustn't" do? How so?

- Can you think of situations where you feel relaxed and at
  ease, comfortable in your skin and utterly free to be
  authentic? How often and when and where do you feel
  this way?
- What are some things you would approach differently in
  your life if you weren't worried about hurting or
  disappointing others?

Please try to answer these questions without judgment or
fear. Your goal for now is simply to collect information.
There is no need to make any changes just yet.

———

Once I realized how much of my life—both the external markers
and my inner landscape—had been a function of letting my social
self call the shots, I experienced a combination of shock and grief,
fascination and hope. I came to see how cut off I had been from my
most vital, energetic, and creative impulses and how disconnected I
had become from some of my deepest values. Under the power of
my social self, I was quick to dismiss all-important things like love
and kindness, contentment and connection. Instead, my self-worth
came from my notions of exceptionalism, hard work, and professional achievement.

It turns out I had it backward all along. Hard work can feel great
and yield tremendous opportunities, and external success can feel
incredibly rewarding. But the *deeper* rewards are often to be found
when we give our essential self the leeway it needs.

To do that, I suggest pausing and returning to the body. Often!
Learning to pay attention to your body's signals can be a lifesaver,
both physically and emotionally. In the same way that pain may be a
sign of illness, tension and tightening let us know when we are doing
(or thinking about) something disagreeable. By contrast, when we
feel light and open, warm, content, energized, or at ease, our essen-

tial selves are saying, "More of this, please!" Learn to listen and, whenever possible, to act accordingly. Use POQR (*pause, observe, question, reflect*) to help you tune in to those sensations and messages throughout the day, something you will get a lot more practice doing in the next chapter. Once you do, you will begin to realize when you are acting from your core beliefs versus the dictates of others.

For example: right now, I am feeling calm, clearheaded, and optimistic about the work I am doing. My heartbeat is steady, my breath is even, my forehead relaxed—all signs that I am feeling patient and at ease. Thirty-five minutes ago, this was not the case at all. Instead, I was tense and stiff, desperately in need of a stretch and struggling to write through a pounding headache and a bout of nausea but unwilling to get up. No wonder, since I had spent much of the day in thrall to my social self, who seemed convinced that completing this book was the key to happiness, or at least the only goal worth pursuing. Never mind that wimpy essential self clamoring for a break!

Then I paused. Because POQR is so ingrained in me, it wasn't long before I spotted my signature pattern. Usually, when I overdo it, it is out of attachment to that old external ideal—that my worth is tied to hard work, or, at least, that work should come before my more essential needs. Then I paused and noticed the pounding headache, my queasiness, the tension in my shoulders and back. Why was I feeling these things? Because I needed to get up from my desk and move! So why wasn't I moving? Because I still had so much work to do before it would be time to pick up my daughter from school. Yet hadn't I learned, time and again, that when I give my essential self just a bit of rest and nurturing, I return to work restored and more productive than when I force myself to trudge through?

Ultimately, I made the decision to get up and stretch. To go downstairs, grab a banana and a glass of water, and go sit in the backyard with the dog. The hiatus was brief but effective and exactly what I needed to make the rest of the day as productive as could be, without feeling sick or miserable in the process.

My social self is sharp and savvy. She knows what it takes to succeed, but her perspective is narrow and her methods overly rigid. To her, even a short rest can feel like failure. Fortunately, she isn't fully in charge anymore. She has learned to yield to an essential self that is not only kinder and gentler, but wiser as well. And she has learned—I have learned—that when they work together, in a balanced way, they make a fantastic team.

NINE

Body of Knowledge

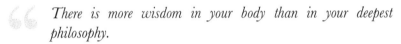

> *There is more wisdom in your body than in your deepest philosophy.*
>
> Friedrich Nietzsche

WHEN WE NEED TO EAT SOMETHING, OUR STOMACH GRUMBLES. When we walk too far in the wrong shoes, our feet ache in protest. When we spend all day hunched over a screen, refusing to take a break, our heads pound, and our vision goes blurry. And as we've seen, when we are mired in unhelpful thinking—*I have to put everyone else first; I'm not tough enough; I suck at technology*—our bodies react quite clearly, too.

In each case, the body is signaling a vital need. It isn't concerned with a number on the scale, the shoe trends of the season, or how much work we are determined to accomplish. Nor does it want us stewing in insecure thoughts. Rather, because it represents the most essential self, it can be trusted to look out for our best interests.

During my coach training, Martha Beck encouraged us to use a tool called the Body Compass to tune in to and abide by our physical messages. And I will never forget the day back in 2014, sitting on the floor of my home office, when I learned to "calibrate" this inner compass and use it to steer my decision-making, much the way sailors navigated the sea in the days before GPS.

Per usual, I was wary of the method at first. As someone who had always had the utmost confidence in my analytical brain, I valued facts over feelings and favored a rational cost-benefit analysis over checking in with my gut. I was much less familiar with (or interested in) "listening to my body," which felt too woo-woo.

But my essential self calmly encouraged me to stay the course. *Maybe it's a silly idea, but it's harmless. What have you got to lose?*

And so I sat myself down with my back propped against the wall, my legs extended in front of me, cautiously following along as my partner, Nicole, guided me over speakerphone through my first Body Compass session. In her soothing and inviting way, she encouraged me to get comfortable and relax, to feel the safety and support of my surroundings, and to breathe deeply in and out. Next, she asked me to think of a recent experience, something stressful or unsettling. "It shouldn't be the worst thing that has ever happened to you, but it should be something that caused you stress, worry, fear, or tension." Nicole asked me to enlist all five senses as I spent a few minutes reliving the scenario in my head, assuring me that we would not talk about the memory. Immediately, my mind went to a recent argument with a friend, a situation where I felt I had been misunderstood and unfairly maligned. After a minute or two, Nicole asked me to describe what I felt in my body—whether there was tightness or pain, dullness or heat, clenching or fluttering, or anything else. She wanted me to be as thorough and specific as I could about what I was feeling and where in my body the sensations appeared.

As I revisited the argument, mentally replaying my friend's hurtful words, I noticed my jaw clenching, my eyes scrunching, and my eyebrows knitting together. It was as if my entire head wanted to close in on itself, the craniofacial equivalent of a fist readying itself to punch. Then I noticed my heart rate rising, my stomach dropping and spinning, my shoulders tightening, everything gripping together in a way that felt entirely familiar, even if I had never taken the time to notice or identify the sensations before.

When Nicole asked me to give this set of sensations a name, I immediately went with "pissed off." When she asked me to rank the feeling state—to give it a number from minus-ten (for the worst I could possibly feel) to plus-ten (the best)—I went with minus-seven. Pretty bad.

Next, Nicole asked me to shake off the unpleasant memory. I stood up, shook out my arms and legs one at a time, did a few shoulder and neck rolls, and gave myself a quick scalp massage. Then I sat back down on the floor for the next step, closing my eyes and taking a few deep breaths in response to Nicole's gentle prompting.

"Recall a recent situation where you felt happy or excited, serene or content, or anything positive at all," she instructed, assuring me that we would not discuss my pleasant memory, that I was meant only to relive and savor it on my own.

I brought to mind an unhurried and carefree day with Rob and the kids, full of warmth and sunshine and no agenda. As Nicole guided me to name the physical sensations I was experiencing, I noticed, with surprise, the *absence* of sensation. Everything that had felt tight, tense, or gripping moments before was now entirely at ease. My heart felt calm, as did my stomach. My shoulders were relaxed, my jaw loose, and my brows relaxed. And then I realized that I was smiling.

In the years since, I have adapted the method into something I call Data Collection, where I encourage clients to analyze and ascertain how their bodies behave in a variety of specific situations, both pleasant and unpleasant. After all, companies collect our data to better understand our needs and improve our consumer experience (not to mention make money from us). Now I'd like to encourage you to try something that will ultimately pay you back: collect some data on yourself. What happens to you physically when you are nervous? What about impatient? Overwhelmed? Content? Excited? Stressed? Uncertain? When you find yourself gripped by self-critical thoughts, how does that manifest in your body? In each situation, how does your body communicate with you?

———

Exercise: Collect Your Data

Data Collection takes the exercises we did in Chapter Two (Reflect on Your Reactions) and combines them with Beck's Body Compass technique to help generate more awareness of your physical tells.

Start by sitting in a way that is comfortable and makes you feel supported. Uncross your arms and legs and get loose. Close your eyes, breathing deeply and evenly until you feel relaxed. Scan your body, without judgment or effort. Notice areas of comfort or discomfort, relaxation or tension. Take a few more deep, calming breaths.

Now, recall a recent situation that caused you to be self-critical or otherwise stressed, fearful, or tense. Some clients feel anxious and insecure, for example, at dinner parties. Others are triggered by upcoming family gatherings, while for others, it tends to be professional demands that test their equanimity. Pick something challenging for you and mentally relive the scenario. Without thinking ahead to what comes next, stay in the memory. Call it up like a movie playing in your mind and completely reinhabit the scene, using whatever senses you can. Linger there. When you are ready, write down any physical sensations you notice. Pinpoint where in your body you feel each sensation. Is it your shoulders, neck, stomach, or face? Anywhere else? Next, note the quality and intensity of the sensation. Is it tight? Gripping? Energizing or draining? How extreme are the sensations? What do you notice? What do you feel?

Now, take another deep breath, shaking out your arms and legs and rolling your head gently. You can even do a little dance—whatever it takes to shed those sensations.
Sit back down and continue breathing with care. This time, I'd like you to repeat the exercise, but with a more pleasant memory. Recall a recent situation where you felt happy, proud, energized, confident, content, or joyful. It might have been a big win at work or a relaxing Sunday at home. Whatever it is, close your eyes and revisit the experience for a minute or two. See yourself in that lovely place.

Once again, scan yourself from head to toe, noting any physical sensations you are experiencing and what is happening in your body. Pay particular attention to areas that were triggered by the previous stressful memory. How do those areas feel now? Record everything that you notice.

Repeat this exercise as often as you like, recalling different scenarios, feeling states, and sensations, and record your discoveries in your notebook. Collect as much data as you can, exploring how your body reflects all manner of thoughts, feelings, and experiences, from proud to ashamed, from irritated to irate to joyful. Ponder what you've learned, and practice paying closer attention to your body's data from now on.

―――――

All three tools—POQR (from Chapter Seven), the Body Compass, and Data Collection—are designed to help you develop more awareness of how your physical body communicates with you.[9] I encourage you to try them all, exploring how they work for you. In my case, using these tools regularly has made me intimately aware of what various physical clues are telling me. Often, these clues are the all too familiar signs of overwork described in the last chapter. There is also the pinching, trapped-in-a-vice sensation in my upper back that means I feel threatened, or the knot in my solar plexus that indicates anxiety. Embarrassment manifests as flutters and warmth, whereas shame washes over fast, prickly, and hot. Confrontation of any kind leads to a racing heart and a flipping stomach, as does presenting a workshop or any form of public speaking (though, thankfully, the sensations disappear rather quickly after I take a few deep breaths). I also know that when I'm feeling content and sure of myself, my entire body feels open and relaxed, while a wide, impossible-to-contain smile means I have stumbled on some painfully obvious truth I have been foolishly resisting or failing to see. This is sometimes followed by a burst of laughter.

I have clients who feel absolutely everything in their face—heat and redness when they are stressed or insecure, a relaxed slackness when all is well. Others notice a tightening in their throat when they have something to say but are afraid to speak up, or an itchy discomfort on their skin when they feel mistrust.

One of my clients, Sarah, feels everything in her chest and has learned that the feeling of her "heart buried in rocks" means she is working too hard or believes she is trapped in some way. Feeling "light and wide open," on the other hand, means she is in balance. Katie, a self-described pleaser, feels a tightening in her back and neck when she feels beholden to people she suspects don't have her best interests at heart.

After tracking and discussing hundreds of physical sensations over the years, I am convinced that the body possesses brilliance. All we have to do is pay attention.

TEN

Ditch It, Delegate It, Do It Up

Truly successful decision-making relies on a balance between deliberate and instinctive thinking.

Malcolm Gladwell

NOW THAT YOU'VE COLLECTED YOUR DATA AND TUNED IN TO YOUR body's "tells"—the not-so-stealthy signals that something is up—what are you going to do with this information?

So much.

Let me tell you about my client Richard, whom we met briefly in Chapter Two and whose "I suck" thinking was some of the worst I have seen as a coach. He initially came to see me because he hoped to better manage his stress and learn to control the angry outbursts he suspected were impacting his success at the office and overall quality of life. He quickly became one of my most eager clients, open to the kind of mind-body work that many of the men I see initially resist.

Despite his arguably "successful" life, including a long, loving marriage, two doting daughters, a solid accounting practice, and an active social life, Richard revealed that he struggled with confidence.

His inner dialogue was as cruel as they come—filled with attacks for his "laziness" or "chubbiness" or "impatient" parenting style. He inevitably began our Monday morning sessions with a long diatribe, detailing some disappointing incident from the previous week and the litany of mental self-criticism that followed.

Just as inevitably, I asked Richard how he had *felt* in those moments. At first, he gave me a blank stare. He could rattle off his negative thoughts without hesitation, but he had no idea what he was feeling in his body. So together, we did multiple versions of the Collect Your Data exercise. At first, he found it incredibly difficult. Repeatedly, I would draw his attention away from his thinking and toward the physical sensations in his body, but as he closed his eyes and imagined himself sitting at his desk and reading a triggering email, all he could notice were the stressful, self-lacerating thoughts circling his mind. With patience and repetition, however, Richard was eventually able to access his physical sensations—the tension in his shoulders and clenching of his jaw, the wave of heat at the back of his neck.

That's when I gave Richard the same assignment I've given you: to use POQR (*pause, observe, question, reflect*) to make it a practice of noticing his body more often. Soon, our Monday mornings were going quite differently. "You'd be so proud of me," he often began. (I love when clients say this; it means they are feeling proud of themselves.) He was practicing being still and going inward, pausing and observing his body and using his breath to calm down. He learned to catch himself slipping into his habitual fight mode and reverse gears before lashing out. By paying attention to his body's physical signs of stress, he was able to implement calming techniques that short-circuited his usual outbursts. The impact was evident. Before shooting off an angry email or blowing up at his daughter—then ruminating in regret—he paused to check in with himself. Little by little, as he realized he was capable of a new response, his confidence grew. Gradually, he felt more competent at work and more patient at home. Colleagues noticed, his family was heartened, and, over time, his blood pressure even dropped. "My doctor asked me what I was doing differently, and I told him I'd hired a life coach," Richard reported with a twinkle in his eye. "I told him you had me paying attention to my body."

After that, I doubled down on my efforts with Richard and everyone else—myself included.

In my law firm days, I used to keep a desk drawer full of nuts and energy bars to help me survive my "just power through" periods. Back then, working insane hours, skipping meals, and barely sleeping were not only part of the gig but also bragworthy. Depriving myself felt vaguely heroic, as if it proved something about my commitment and work ethic. Now that I've gotten into the habit of checking in with my body multiple times a day and honoring what it has to say, I've found that it almost never wants an energy bar.

As was the case with Richard, sometimes focusing on my body has proved crucial to my health—like a few years ago, when I felt unusually fatigued and foggy, went to my doctor, and was diagnosed with Lyme disease at the earliest possible stage. More often, the signals herald something less dire but, in my opinion, equally important. The small ways we neglect or abuse ourselves on a daily basis can take a massive cumulative toll, physically and emotionally. We all know that stress has been linked to countless health conditions—from heart disease to diabetes to allergies to migraine headaches. And while some amount of stress is inevitable, much of it is avoidable. By simply trusting our body's needs and nurturing ourselves in the tiniest ways, we can reap major dividends, not just physically, but in terms of making better decisions.

This brings me to one of my favorite exercises, something I call the 3-D Approach. It's a method I've adapted ever so slightly from Martha Beck's Bag It, Barter It, Better It tool, which we trainees were encouraged to use ourselves and with our clients whenever *anything* registered as less than ideal on the Body Compass.[10] For almost ten years now, I've personally turned to this tool whenever I find myself dreading a task, avoiding responsibility, or feeling unenthusiastic about upcoming plans. It involves pausing (of course), then asking myself three questions: *Can I ditch it? Can I delegate it? Can I do it up?*

Sounds easy, right? Now take a minute to review your calendar or to-do list. Identify anything you have coming up in the next week or month that makes you feel less than thrilled. It could be a presentation at work or a family wedding, an important email you need to send or even just a coffee date with a friend. Looking at my own calendar, I see that I have upcoming dinner plans with my old friend, Jen, on what is supposed to be a gorgeous day. This is registering as a definite plus-ten throughout my body. I feel nothing but lightheartedness and joy as I picture the two of us laughing about old times. By contrast, I'm scheduled for gum surgery in two weeks, a definite minus-ten. As I envision myself sitting in the periodontist's chair, cotton wads shoved between my lips and jaw, the buzzing of the tools in my ears, I want to cry. My throat and chest tighten, and my heartbeat accelerates in anticipation of pain. I feel both nauseated and heavy, but also avoidant, searching for potential excuses and reasons to postpone.

In the case of my dinner with Jen, the only move is to savor and enjoy our dinner and be grateful for the friendship. But when it comes to oral surgery, it's less clear what I can do to tamp down the dread.

Taking the 3-D Approach, I ask myself, *Can I ditch it?* Well, I'd like to, but if I continue to ignore the problem, I will likely lose a tooth—meaning that I have to go through with this surgery, as awful as it will be. Here's where things get interesting. In the case of my surgery—or anything unpleasant that feels like a "must do"—I ask myself (and you) to think twice. Is it really true that I "have to" get this surgery? Am I absolutely sure that I "can't" ditch the whole thing? What would happen if I canceled?

What's surprising is that simply considering whether options exist can make us feel better—and the truth is, we usually have more choices than we appreciate. The trouble is, we tend to be so burdened by guilt, obligation, or inertia that we don't recognize them. And when we look at unpleasant tasks as inevitable, whether getting surgery, showing up for work, remaining in an unhappy relationship, or attending Thanksgiving dinner, we often end up feeling like passive victims in our own life, letting "have-tos" control us.

(Remember the social self I talked about in Chapter Eight? These rules come from that part of you.) When things feel forced upon us, when we feel we have no choices, we tend to get resentful and angry. We feel trapped.

In contrast, making conscious choices is empowering and energizing. By viewing our decisions as volitional rather than imposed upon us, we feel liberated. No matter what the situation, if you make the effort to pause and remind yourself that you *can* say no— even if you don't—you will feel lighter and stronger.

Repeat after me: *We almost always have choices.* The trick is to recognize that our choices carry consequences, like losing a tooth, so we need to consider those, too, and whether we are willing to accept them.

Ultimately, you may decide that ditching it isn't worth it. Yet because you've actively made the decision to move forward, I promise you will feel more like an engaged participant in your life rather than a passive victim. That, in turn, can significantly impact your level of happiness. Psychologists who study well-being have determined that feelings of agency—when we perceive that we have some control over our environment—are essential for well-being. By contrast, having low decision latitude (an inability to make decisions or influence outcomes) has been correlated with lower levels of well-being.[11]

Now to the second question in the 3-D Approach: *Can I delegate it?* That is, can someone else do it for you, whether a colleague, a helpful friend, or someone you might hire? If your answer is a knee-jerk "no way!" again, take the time to rethink your reaction.

In the case of my oral surgery, no one could stand in for me, obviously. But I know so many people who take on project after project, lamenting how overwhelmed they feel but never considering what they might offload. If you can afford to delegate—or find another way to enlist some help and lighten your load—why not do so?

My favorite thing to delegate is feeding my family, a task I used to find entirely oppressive. Add up my desire to please my picky eaters and my self-imposed pressure to provide nutritious, balanced, and creative meals, and the thought of walking into the kitchen to prep yet another meal made me want to scream. Occasionally, I did.

Which is why I turned to the 3-D Approach. *Could I ditch the cooking-dinner thing?* Once I asked myself this question, I realized immediately how happy it would make me to do exactly that and never think about family dinners again. But the consequences—letting my children starve to death—seemed rather unacceptable.

Then I thought about the delegation piece…and realized there was a wealth of options I'd never considered. When I bothered to ask my husband whether he'd pitch in, it turned out he was happy to do the cooking a few nights a week. On other nights, no one seemed to mind if we got takeout or prepared foods from the supermarket. And when I did cook, I stuck with tried-and-true meals I knew everyone liked, ditching any pressure on myself to be creative. Now, when I'm in the mood, I try something more adventurous but keep my expectations realistic (and backup pizza in the freezer). Thanks to the 3-D Approach, I no longer feel saddled with this daily burden, and I have much more time to devote to other priorities. I also feel less resentful of the people I love and far more relaxed and engaged when we all sit down to eat together.

The third question to ask yourself is *Can I do it up?* If you won't (or can't) ditch or delegate, this is your opportunity to get imaginative and see if you can make the experience even slightly more pleasant. After all, just because you are determined to *do* something doesn't mean you must do so miserably. Can you give yourself a small reward for completing the task? Might you change the timing to make it more convenient? Can you pair it with another activity, like listening to an audiobook, to add some distraction or lift your mood? During my oral surgery, I put on headphones to block out the buzzing tools and listened to a favorite podcast. The experience still wasn't pleasant, but the point is, it's possible to make almost anything more tolerable.

In my experience, *doing it up* is especially helpful when it comes to all the daily obligations and responsibilities we tend to push our way through, unwittingly racing the clock or aiming to please others. And it is so simple. Just slow down. Pause and breathe.

Observe the pressure you are feeling (or the unhelpful, possibly perfectionist thinking that's driving it), and then cut yourself a little slack. It will only take a moment but will allow you to continue doing whatever you are doing in a more enjoyable, less onerous way. Why not give it a try?

I also used the 3-D Approach with my client Dr. K., the over-whelmed cardiologist who felt as if she were on a hamster wheel and couldn't keep up. After we exposed her inner critic and explored the limiting beliefs and painful thoughts that were making her life feel so challenging, we turned to the 3-D's to figure out how she might find some relief.

We started with *Can I ditch it?*, the "it" being her cardiology practice. The consequences—abandoning her patients and sacri-ficing her livelihood—were nonstarters (no surprise there). But when we moved on to the *delegate* options, Dr. K. admitted that for years, she'd thought about hiring an associate to share her workload but had been too consumed by her day-to-day busyness to pursue this path. As we talked this through, the faulty logic of "I'm too busy to seek support, so I'll just keep doing what I'm doing while continuing to suffer" became plain. Believing she had no time to help herself was robbing her of her passion for medicine and taking a toll on her well-being. Meanwhile, when she seriously thought about *delegating* some of her responsibilities to another physician, she immediately felt a wave of relief. We could have stopped there, but just for fun, I asked Dr. K. how she might *do it up*. That's when she floated the idea, the "dream," of taking a few afternoons off each week to get the much needed "me time" she craved, something that would become a reality once she had a partner.

And indeed, after bringing on another physician, Dr. K. told me she felt less overwhelmed at work and was also getting the time off she craved without neglecting her patients. And though she is making less money, the loss in income feels worth it. She told me recently, "I am still earning enough, and at this point in my life, time feels more valuable to me than money." Dr. K. recognized the pain she was in and was willing to *pause*, make some frank *observations* about her life, ask herself some probing *questions*, *reflect* honestly, and then take action.

Dr. K.'s story is a personal favorite of mine, and not only because it has such a happy ending. Rather, it exemplifies how our inner critics and the limiting beliefs they spew can weigh us down and keep us stuck, whereas pausing, clarifying, and confronting those beliefs can energize us in new and unexpected ways. Once Dr. K. took the time to articulate the unspoken rules by which she lived and to connect those attitudes with her lack of energy and enthusiasm, she was better positioned to explore new possibilities and make some changes.

Are you willing to do the same?

ELEVEN

The Inner Knowing

 Pay attention to the whispers so you won't have to listen to the screams.

Cherokee proverb

IMAGINE YOURSELF OUT FOR A DRIVE, PUZZLING OVER SOME PROBLEM, when, suddenly, you are struck by a moment of truth. Call it an urge or a tug, an "aha!" or a lightbulb moment, but to me, it's an unmistakable sensation of *knowing*. At times it might be subtle, a vague hunch that you'd be better off going left instead of right, though you can't explain why. Or it may be a more powerful sense of absolute certainty in place of confusion, which may at first feel surprising but then seem totally obvious.

Some refer to this inner knowing as intuition or a higher self. Some call it the soul.

I call my inner knowing "Leah."

Go ahead and name yours, too.

We are all born with an inner knowing, the more compassionate counterbalance to our inner critic. Think of this knowing as another little voice inside, possibly the voice of your essential self, more prone to gentle reassurance than heated warnings. If your inner critic is a badgering bully, full of ambition or largely motivated by fear, then your inner knowing is a benevolent bestie: loving, wise, and wanting nothing but the best for you. If your inner critic cares only about keeping you safe from humiliation, your inner knowing is guided by genuine concern for your health, happiness, and overall well-being.

Meet Leah

I always imagine Leah as an older woman with timeless elegance. In my mind, I see her deep-set brown eyes, long, silvery blonde hair, and warm smile. Leah's movements are unrushed and graceful, and she exudes an immutable, natural beauty. Her energy is calming and supportive rather than overbearing or aggressive. She is a willing, gentle guide who loves me unconditionally and never resorts to shoulding or shaming. She is like an experienced first grade teacher combined with a trusted friend combined with an always-on-my-side fairy godmother.

Unlike fearful Lola, who alternates between petulant child, sullen teenager, and evil queen, Leah remains serene and unflappable. She never says, "I told you so," or utters a single harsh word. She simply remains calm and carries on, confident that I will eventually find my way without her needing to interfere too much.

"Knowing" goes beyond collecting data points, possessing information, or assessing benefits and costs. Knowing is a sensation, a moment of absolute certainty that starts—you guessed it—in the body. If your physical reaction to your inner critic is to tense up, the physical experience of inner knowing is the opposite. For me, those powerful moments of clarity and certainty are apt to feel solid yet open, free, and full of possibility.

Of course, everyone's body behaves differently in moments of knowing, so it's important to learn to read your own signals and let them guide you. For some, the inner knowing lives in the chest or heart; for others, the throat or stomach. Perhaps you get a tingly sensation when you think about spending time with a certain someone. Maybe you feel a rush of calm and comfort when you imagine finally making some long-dreamed-of move, or you feel loose and open, strong and centered as you arrive at a moment of decision. Many clients describe an overall feeling of release and liberation. Of *just* being themselves. Whatever your body's signals, noticing them takes attention, awareness, and trust, which is why I recommend using POQR (from Chapter Seven) or the Data Collection exercise (from Chapter Nine) to establish what knowing feels like for you.

For me, knowing always starts in my heart and radiates outward in concentric circles. In that moment, all the competing voices battling in my mind fall silent, allowing a subtle but sure truth to break through. I feel myself slowly exhale, as if I'm releasing something, though I may not have even realized I was holding my breath. Then my face is overtaken by that enormous, too-big-to-be-contained smile I referred to earlier. It's the opposite of a poker face because I have nothing to hide, and I wouldn't be capable if I tried. It's the smile of certainty.

Still, despite all Leah has to offer, for a long time, I barely noticed her. That's because our doubts and insecurities have a way of screaming for our attention, drowning out our inner knowing and obscuring their presence. After all, Western culture can be dismissive of intuition versus cold, hard facts. Very few of us are taught how to tap into or trust our intuitive knowledge. When we are trying to solve a problem or make a big decision, our tendency is to create spreadsheets, analyze the pros and cons, think through every permutation. That's important, of course, but pausing to go inward and listen to your inner knowing is crucial too.

———

AT TWENTY-SEVEN, I was just a year out of law school and at the height of my "work hard/play hard" phase of life. Long days at the office were usually followed by late nights out, when I'd blow off steam until the wee hours, then head home for a little sleep before doing it all again the next day. It was fun, fabulous, a bit wild, sexy, and adventurous.

It was also lonely.

I never admitted that, even to myself. Instead, I stayed in motion. As determined as I was to succeed in my career, I was equally focused on racking up experience and living my life to the fullest. At the time, that meant clubbing and partying, taking advantage of all that New York City had to offer. A cousin visiting from Florida once commented that my life was like a live version of *Sex and the City*, and I smiled to myself. *Of course it is,* I thought. *I wouldn't have it any other way.*

Then things began to shift.

One night, I came home late after yet another evening out carousing with friends. As I entered my bedroom, instead of collapsing into bed, I suddenly paused in front of my dresser. I remember feeling as if something was gently tugging at my attention, pointing me toward the framed dusty photos that had been there for so many years I no longer really noticed them. That night, I found myself picking up a very old snapshot of my family, all of us dressed up and posing by the azalea bushes in front of my childhood home. My mother was tan and regal-looking in a silk burgundy dress; my father was dashing in a gray three-piece suit, his arm around my mother's waist. As for me, I looked utterly secure nestled between them, my dark hair in braids, my wide smile marked by two missing front teeth. I must have been around five, which was before everything went sideways for our family. Back then, I remember feeling innocent and pure. I wasn't striving for anything but was happy *just being.*

Enter Leah.

Standing there gazing at that old photo is one of the first times I became aware of my inner knowing, though it would still be years before I gave the feeling a name. What I experienced in that moment—what I felt bubbling up from deep within—was total calm, coupled with a question: *How are you going to get from here to there?* As the words formed in my head, I suddenly felt released, seen, and recognized, as if I had been reunited with the little girl in the photograph who valued family and love, connection and simplicity. In that stillness, Leah kindly pointed out that I wasn't honoring my values or living in a way that felt healthy or true. Instead, I'd been consumed by the chase—of career, of partying—pursuits that had always felt electric and exciting and adventurous. But staring at the picture, it struck me that all along, I had taken for granted that my ideal early childhood—stable and sweet, loving and family-centered —would also be my future. Suddenly, thinking about how I was spending my time, I wasn't so sure where I was headed.

How are you going to get from here to there?

Leah, I know now, wanted me to remember who I really was, and what I cared about most, before it was too late. The little girl in the photograph knew what was most important to her, and apparently, she was still there inside of me, patiently waiting to have her say with the hard-working, hard-partying twentysomething striver I'd become. She was waiting until I was ready to listen.

Things started to change dramatically after that.

Just a few weeks later, I met the man who would become my husband. He was another attorney at my very large firm, a well-regarded partner in another practice area, someone I knew of but had never officially met. One day, we happened to be seated next to each other at a lunch, and we began chatting. That's when my inner knowing whispered in my ear again.

I feel like I could be anywhere with him right now, like we should never stop talking.

I hadn't expected much from this work lunch, and I certainly wasn't planning to fall for a colleague, let alone a partner. But as the conversation continued, a calm, reassuring comfort settled over me, a certainty that something important was happening.

Later that day, I visited my mother in the hospital. When I walked into her room, she was sitting up, playing blackjack on the bed with my brother, looking much better than she had since cancer surgery—her first go-round—a few days earlier. I gave her a quick kiss, happy to see her looking more like herself, and also feeling kind of giddy.

"*What?*" she said, after taking one look at me.

"Nothing," I lied.

"I know you," she went on. "What's up?"

"I think I might have a crush on someone at work," I fessed up.

"I knew it!" she laughed. Then, "Go for it, honey!"

My mother's name was Leah.

Over the years, my inner Leah has established quite an impressive résumé of personal triumphs. Despite the excessive attention I gave Lola and the outward achievements she demanded, all along, it was Leah who had been keeping my most essential needs in mind. She had been the one encouraging me to honor my deepest values, to be easier on myself, and to keep my priorities in order. In fact, had Leah not shown up when she did—had I continued to let Lola run my personal show—everything I cherish about my life today might never have come to be.

Finding your version of Leah requires stillness and attentiveness, what some might call mindful attention. If you pause and let yourself sit in the stillness, you'll find that the voice is always there—tireless, devoted, and true. That voice may not sound like Leah, or even like anyone at all. Just as you explored the specific bodily sensations alerting you to the presence of your inner critic, you'll want to try to do the same for your inner knowing. Maybe what you notice is a tug or nudge in a particular direction. For some, there are visual images —like a flash of a dream—that feel like messages or signs.

To help you identify your version of inner knowing, reflect back on any "How am I going to get from here to there?" moments or eureka revelations of your own. How and when did they arrive? What happened next? Then dive into the exercise below.

————

Exercise: Access Your Inner Knowing

Get present and still, giving yourself a break from the busyness of daily concerns. Without overthinking, try to recall a moment of clarity—any situation where you were struck with absolute certainty, guided by a deep sense of knowing.

Where were you? What were you doing or thinking? And, most important, what did it feel like? Try to channel the memory and embody yourself as you were at that time.

Next, close your eyes and revisit the scene. Scan your body and your senses. What do you feel, physically? What can you see around you; what can you touch, hear, smell, or taste?

If nothing comes to mind at first, be patient. Given the quiet and gentle way our inner knowing can express itself, it may be tough to recognize it at first. Still, try to be as specific as possible as you identify how *your* inner knowing shows up for *you*. Do you feel as if you've been stopped in your tracks, or, as one client described, "jolted awake from a dreamlike state, thrust from distraction to presence"? Maybe you feel goosebumps on your skin or a settled feeling in your heart. Or perhaps it is *just* a feeling that all is right in your world—your whole body saying *Yes! This is exactly where I want to be right now*. Pay attention to these sensations and welcome them in the future.

————

If that exercise felt difficult, rest assured that daily practices like meditation, walking in nature, or anything that allows you to feel open, relaxed, and trusting will deepen your connection to your inner knowing. Freewriting can also help, especially when done by hand. Just keep your pen moving, allowing an unedited stream of consciousness to flow onto the page for ten or fifteen minutes, and notice the nuggets of truth that emerge. Or simply take a break from busyness and turn off your gadgets, then ground yourself in the present moment, focusing on the breath. But the very best way to access this wise inner force is to regularly check in with your physical self, using your body as a guide as you move through your days. Whether you stick with the tools I've offered (POQR, Data Collection, and the Body Compass) or you prefer to design your own approach, please know this: paying attention to your body and the various ways it communicates with you is a life-changing skill. Trust it to let you know when you are moving in the right direction and acting in your genuine best interests. Trust it, too, when it suggests you may be pushing or forcing something or bowing to your inner critic or any other social dictates instead of honoring your essential self.

Learning to distance yourself from your inner critic and all the negativity and fear it spews, while also learning to heed your inner knowing, is a tried-and-true formula for living well. Not that your version of Lola won't occasionally overpower your Leah; that's normal, and it's perfectly OK. We're human. We slow down to witness the mangled, twisted wreck of a car accident but cruise past hundreds of intact cars without a thought. We regale friends with the dramatic saga of a vacation gone wrong but barely say a word when all was lovely and smooth. We vent about the ways people disappoint us while never mentioning their more positive attributes. Our negativity bias ensures we are likely to be more enthralled with the juicy disaster than a pleasant but seemingly ordinary event. As I've said earlier, human beings are wired this way—to focus on negativity—for survival.

Then again, there is so much more to life than merely surviving. Your inner knowing wants you to *thrive*. She knows who you are, at your core, as well as what you *truly* want and need. She won't resort to coercion or manipulation; instead, she'll tell you plainly with soft, unwavering confidence what she thinks is best. Pay attention. Listen to her whispers. Feel her presence and allow it to guide you.

TWELVE

Painful Personal Patterns and Their Larger Impact

 Nothing is permanent about our behavior patterns except our belief that they are so.

Moshe Feldenkrais

ONE OF MY FAVORITE *PEANUTS* CARTOONS SHOWS SNOOPY AND Charlie Brown sitting on a dock on a bright sunny day, looking out across a lake at the horizon. The bubble over Charlie Brown's head says, "Someday, we are all going to die, Snoopy." Snoopy's response? "True, but on all the other days, we will not."

I include this cartoon in my workshops because it's playful but also because it so beautifully captures how the lens through which you view your world colors your experience—how two individuals can gaze at the exact same scene but see things very differently. Snoopy tends to dance and skip through life. Charlie Brown? Not so much.

So … are you a Snoopy or a Charlie Brown?

To use a real-life example, my husband and I were recently stuck in bumper-to-bumper traffic. He felt irritated about the delay, sighing with exasperation every thirty seconds, constantly checking the GPS map to see how far the red traffic lines extended, turning to Waze in search of alternate routes, and doing a lot of unintelligible grumbling. As for me, I didn't want to be stuck in traffic either, but I recognized that our current situation was beyond our control. Even if we could map another route on Waze, we weren't going anywhere for the foreseeable future.

I haven't always reacted with such equanimity. A few years ago, I would have been just as aggravated as my husband. In fact, at the beginning of that traffic jam, when our smooth ride first came to a halt, I *was* just as aggravated as Rob. My muscles tensed, and the car felt small and hot, even slightly claustrophobic. Unhelpful thoughts like *I have no time for this!* and *Uggggh, why didn't we leave earlier?* surfaced instantaneously. Luckily, the pity party was short-lived. Almost immediately, I recognized my own Charlie Brown tendencies—a painful personal pattern consisting of two threads, *Never Enough Time* and *Always All My Fault*—and could course-correct on the spot.

Once I caught myself slipping into that frame of mind, I paused and took a deep breath. Then I reminded myself to think twice (Chapter Four)—to remember that it was not necessarily the traffic but my attitude *about* the traffic that would determine my mood. I made the conscious decision to turn my thoughts elsewhere. I started with gratitude, appreciating that we were safe in the car, not lying mangled on the side of the road. As Rob grumbled on, I took comfort in the fact that we would arrive home in one piece, even if late.

Same situation, different interpretation, different experiences. Snoopy versus Charlie Brown.

What are your painful personal patterns? How does your penchant for self-criticism—or your tendency to take things personally, to blame others, or any other pattern—diminish your experience of life? What would it look and feel like if you let that go?

Challenges will always arise in life; they're inevitable, just like traffic jams. Our initial habitual reactions—anger, dejection, self-recrimination, or avoidance—may feel inevitable as well. Where we have the opportunity to change things, however, is in our ability to choose. To choose autopilot or to take the wheel. To choose to clarify and confront what's bothering us or to drift along and let it sink our mood. To choose the path of least resistance or to redirect our attention and widen our perspective.

Remember, your thoughts are the driving force behind many of your most stressful experiences and painful personal patterns. Our feelings aren't caused by a traffic jam (or a rainy day or any other circumstance). At least, not entirely. Rather, it is your thinking in that moment—*This is so typical of my horrible luck!* versus *Thank goodness we're safe!*—that determines mood, behavior, and our resulting experiences. The key is to learn how to catch your moods and reactivity, to pause and breathe and question your thinking. And even when you find yourself in a situation you cannot change—your partner wants a divorce, your boss is letting you go, your doctor has harrowing news—as difficult as it may be, recognize that you still have choices. You can *choose* acceptance. You can *choose* to somehow get something out of the experience. Acceptance is a powerful tool, and one that's well worth honing along with the other concepts we've explored so far. Keeping all that in mind, I would like to ask you to pause and ponder one question:

Is your negative thinking serving you well?

I was first asked this question during coach training, and it shook me to my core—and helped me to see Lola in a whole new way. For so long, I had been crediting her with giving me an advantage in life, helping me to stay sharp, to maintain my edge. With that one question, I suddenly saw her negativity for what it was: unnecessary, unhelpful, and even, sometimes, abusive. I had turned myself into a racehorse and let Lola assume the role of jockey, riding me hard and wielding the reins. She was perennially on my back, always slapping me in the ass and pushing me to reach further and run faster.

The trouble was, there was no finish line in sight.

I would never, ever get there.

My need for constant motion and productivity and my inability to rest was a painful personal pattern, driven entirely by my "Do More, Be More (or else you suck)" story. It was *not* serving me well.

It was making me feel stressed and impatient, agitated, ineffective, and irritable.

It was also the ultimate act of self-sabotage.

I was so consumed with maximizing my potential, I neglected to honor some of my best qualities—my ability to love, to connect deeply with others, to be a nurturer, supporter, and friend. These were qualities I readily celebrated in others but could not seem to value in myself. Instead, I was always focusing on some elusive future, prioritizing "there and then" over "here and now." With all that narrowly focused rushing around in pursuit of *better* and *different* and *more*, I was squandering my time and my potential, the exact result I was trying to avoid.

I've since noticed this pattern in many of my clients as well. Just like them, I was sitting in my dirty diaper.

If that metaphor makes you wrinkle your nose, stay with me for a minute. Think about Charlie Brown and his less-than-rosy view of life. Why does he hold on to it? How does it benefit him? Perhaps it is an attempt to manage expectations, to anticipate the inevitable disappointments in life and brace for them. Many of my clients report exactly this approach. They conflate pessimism with self-protection, as if maintaining a negative worldview shields them from pain. When I press them, however, time and again they come to see the pitfalls in this approach—because no amount of anticipation ever blunts the impact of a future blow. All it does is detract from the time we could have been enjoying all along.

Imagine a jealous husband who loves his wife but is terrified of losing her. His fear makes him overly controlling. He can't bring himself to trust her. She is patient and understanding, but his jealousy becomes increasingly oppressive. She puts up with it for as long as she can, telling herself that it is just his way, that it comes from love. Meanwhile, every day the jealous husband peppers her with questions. *Where are you going? Why do you need to go out? Who else is going to be there?* Eventually, his wife feels resentful. She stops telling him what she is doing. Their marriage falters.

The jealous husband is sitting in his dirty diaper. On the surface, he has exactly what he wants in life, which is his beloved wife. Yet because he is plagued by his fear of losing her, he tenses and tightens, ever vigilant and aware of the possibility of that loss instead of savoring their time together in the here and now. His strategy for protecting against a future he dreads—the one where she leaves him—is bound to bring it about. Doubtless, his worries feel like a safeguard against some future danger to be avoided at all costs. But in fact, he is constantly dwelling in a steaming pile of his worst-case scenario. And he is bringing it upon himself, first by living with the painful feelings caused by his imagination, and eventually, in reality.

Similarly, my client Monica struggled to see her pattern of sabotaging what she wanted most: a solid relationship. A thirty-three-year-old graphic designer with a short brown bob and almond-shaped eyes, Monica was outgoing, with a wry, self-deprecating humor. She reached out to me to get some clarity and support around her romantic life. As Monica filled me in on her dating history and the men and women with whom she'd recently been involved, it was clear that meeting people wasn't a problem for her. She had had plenty of relationships. But after a few months of jittery excitement and hope, things would inevitably start to go wrong. Monica would begin to feel unseen and unheard, unappreciated and disrespected. She told me that after a while, she felt lonelier inside a relationship than she did when she was on her own.

"No one gets me," she complained, understandably sad and frustrated. "Not the men. Not the women. Not anyone."

Monica was wise enough to recognize a pattern on her part. "If it had happened just once or twice, I could chalk it up to the other person's selfishness or inability to compromise—or some other flaw on their part. But one after the other, they say they love me, and I don't *feel* that love. It's as if they love a version of me that isn't real—someone self-sufficient and capable, always available to meet their needs, always operating on their wavelength, but not entitled to any needs of her own. And when I try to assert myself, whoever I'm with seems to get disillusioned, and everything falls apart. What am I doing wrong?"

As we narrowed in on her most recent relationship, it became evident that in the early days, Monica's entire focus was on "getting" the beau—which she did pretty easily, given her knack for reading people and assessing how to secure their interest. As soon as she felt attracted to someone, and without even realizing she was doing it, she proceeded as if she were interviewing for a job, giving all the answers that would earn her the gig. As for being who she truly needed to be—herself—that was a bigger challenge, especially since her inner critic constantly warned: *You have to be who they want and need you to be, otherwise you'll be alone.*

And so, she presented an edited version of herself to any potential mate—someone who eagerly accommodated that person's tastes and interests but rarely expressed her own, always acquiescing to their restaurant choices or ideas for weekend plans. She told herself that this was what it meant to be "laid back" and that she was "happy to compromise." And she was, to a point. But eventually, she felt unable to show her true self, and her resentment built until she *had* to make her true desires known, often in a way that sent the other person running.

Eventually, through our discussions, she came to recognize and understand how she was sabotaging herself, trying to connect with someone who would love and appreciate her for who she was by twisting herself into a pleasing, accommodating chameleon. "Oh my God!" she gasped. "How *could* anyone really get me when I've never honestly shown up in the first place?"

And so, we delved deeper into her pattern of behavior. We began, as always, by pausing and breathing. Next, we fleshed out and clarified Monica's deeply held beliefs about relationships. She harbored a few classics: *I need to be in a relationship to be happy; better to secure the relationship first and worry about improving it later; being involved with someone is better than being alone, even if it doesn't feel that way.*

Then I asked her that one simple question: *Is this thinking serving you well?*

Suddenly, it seemed obvious how misguided her behavior had been. But before I go on to discuss the tools Monica used to confront and change her painful personal patterns—and how you can begin to move beyond yours—let's take a moment to check in by getting still. Think back to the questions I asked you in Chapter

Three. *What do you yearn to achieve? What is your dream vision for your life? What gets in your way?* Again and again, I've found that more than any other obstacle, it's our limiting beliefs and various "I suck" thoughts that block us from achieving things that are very much within our reach.

———

Exercise: Connect the Dots

Revisit your Greatest Hits from Chapter Two and select one painful thought on which to focus. Do you believe you're too needy or too quick to anger? Do you tell yourself you are not smart enough or interesting enough? Do you dislike your appearance? Are you single but telling yourself you need to be in a relationship to be happy? Are you in a relationship but telling yourself you want out? Or are your personal critiques more work-related?

For now, identify just one of your painful thoughts. It shouldn't be your harshest thought, but something that nags at you and makes you feel like you suck in some way. Next, work through the questions below:

- What is the painful thought?
- What is the common trigger?
- What is your usual reaction?
- What is the direct impact?
- What is the bigger impact?
- And finally, is this thinking serving you well?

———

I have struggled with some painful personal patterns of my own over the years, one of the biggest being my relationship to writing. As much as I have always loved to express myself on the page, Lola repeatedly insists that I "suck" at writing, viewing the activity as "indulgent," "pointless," and "far better left to the *real* writers." This thinking pops up whenever I put pen to page or even *think* about writing something. Whenever I consider sharing my work, Lola gets especially heated, bringing to mind the firing squad of naysayers who will dismiss me because *If you don't have anything earth-shattering and original to say, don't bother*. The result is that I feel paralyzed, small, and totally shut down, my mind swirling with regrets about every "bad" decision I've made in the past. My brow furrows, my shoulders hunch, my energy wanes. Instead of writing, I get busy doing other "more productive" things. And still, the writing ideas continue to come, though until recently, I never got further than scribbling away in notebooks or crafting essays and blog posts that were seen only by me. All of this made me feel sorry for myself, which really ticked Lola off—*No pity parties allowed!*—and so I'd turn my focus to billing or marketing or emptying the dishwasher. When I was truly dispirited, I'd scroll through social media and admire all the *other* people doing amazing things in the world while I sat around feeling lousy about myself.

How's that for a painful personal pattern?

I see so many of these same patterns in my clients, like James, a marketing expert with over thirty years of experience in the corporate world. A self-made man who climbed his way from working-class roots to the Ivy League to some of the best-known companies on the planet, James is undeniably successful. Creative, dedicated, and hardworking, he is passionate about the work he does helping businesses build their brands and optimize performance. Unfortunately, despite all his success helping others, James would routinely get stuck when it came to marketing his own work. Each time he attempted to post on social media, network with colleagues or toot his own horn in any way (the triggers), his inner critic, playfully named Little John Wayne, piped up. Loudly! Painful "I suck" thoughts like *If I were any good, I wouldn't need to market myself* or *Advertising my services makes me look desperate* consistently got in his way, which he knew was illogical—and ironic—given what he did for a living. Fortunately, once we took a closer look at the pattern, James came to see both the direct impact (feeling stymied, insecure, frustrated, and overall lousy) as well as the larger impact (holding himself back, damaging his business prospects and his bottom line). From there, he began to implement some new, more supportive strategies (which we will explore in Chapters Fifteen and Sixteen) to help bust up that unhelpful pattern.

Or take Jordanna, a junior partner at a major law firm who came to me hoping I could help her shore up her confidence. Despite having recently made partner, Jordanna doubted herself. "It's a sharp-elbows kind of place," she told me. "You are only as good as your last deal. I have to be on 110 percent of the time, and still, I worry that's not enough. I used to feel proud of my accomplishments and fairly confident about my intelligence and work ethic, but suddenly, I don't. My partners make me feel like I can never stop proving myself."

It was the phrase "make me feel" that caught my attention.

All too often, it seems as if our siblings, bosses, partners, friends —sometimes even strangers—"make" us feel things. But much like all of those "shoulds" and "musts," "shouldn'ts" and "can'ts," whenever someone else "makes" you feel anything, it's a golden opportunity to dig in and reassess. Because no one can "make" you feel badly about something that you don't believe to be true about yourself.

———

Exercise: They Make Me Feel

Imagine yourself sitting at lunch with a colleague or friend. Out of nowhere, she looks at you with a disgusted face and accuses you of being purple. "I can't believe you," she says. "How can you sit there, unapologetic and self-assured, when you are so purple? How dare you!?"

Now, reflect on how this would make you feel. My guess is you would feel confused. You might start to question whether you had heard correctly, or whether your dining companion was suffering some sort of psychotic episode. "What are you talking about?" you might ask. You would perceive the apparent insult as nonsensical and ridiculous. It would not land or cause you any pain because of your certainty that you are definitely not purple.

Now imagine the same scenario, except that your lunch date turns to you and somehow insinuates that you have been selfish or irresponsible, lazy or stupid or anything that might appear on your inner critic's Greatest Hits list. Perhaps she is attacking you directly; perhaps it's simply her tone that seems to confirm your worst fears about yourself. Now how do you feel?

Can you notice the difference? Can you feel the connection between your painful reaction and your own personal beliefs?

―――――

In my experience, the feeling of being exposed, slighted, or diminished only arises when you agree, even ever so slightly, that you suck. Once again, it's all about clarifying and confronting your own beliefs. Think of the moment as an invitation to get still and clarify why the interaction (or the relationship) is causing you discomfort, then do some work from there. Is what they are "making" you feel entirely their fault? Is there something you also believe to be true, some painful thought about yourself that is worth confronting?

For those of us who are especially self-critical, we rarely need others to "make" us feel badly. Like Sierra, a lifelong friend of mine who comes from a musical family and, as a child, loved to sing, dance, act, and play the piano. After college, life did its thing, and she shifted away from the arts to a safer, more predictable career in event planning, putting her old life and loves behind her.

Recently, though, after a nasty health scare, she called me.

"I want to get back on the stage," she said. "I want to sing again."

"Fantastic!" I replied. "Where can I see you perform?"

"Ha!" she laughed.

"Why *ha*?"

It turns out that for years, Sierra had a lot of stories running through her head that had been blocking her return to music. Overcoming her illness gave her new motivation—that new-lease-on-life feeling that makes us want to throw our arms wide open and pursue our most essential dreams before it's too late. At the same time, Sierra's inner critic kicked into high gear. *That's not practical. You'll just embarrass yourself (and your family). You're not a real artist. Plus, between work and family, you're already so busy—how do you expect to fit in one more thing?*

Sierra's struggle reminded me of a popular saying I first heard during coach training: "The mind is a wonderful servant, but a terrible master."

This quote has been attributed to a number of different people, and when I first heard it, I didn't get it. But as I spent more time examining and questioning my thoughts and helping clients do the same, I came to understand its deeper meaning. The mind is unruly. It wanders. It conjures up worries, shouts warnings, and overwhelms us with concerns. To quote Daniel Goleman again, "the worrying mind spins on in an endless loop of low-grade melodrama, one set of concerns leading on to the next and back again."[12] All of this is part of our survival instinct, of course, our ever-present need to control the environment and keep ourselves safe.

But is safety the only goal? Don't we also want love and happiness, creative expression, fulfillment, and success? The truth is the instincts that have helped us to survive over the centuries can also make it difficult for us to pursue our dreams and truly thrive.

Sierra's inner critic was the ultimate "terrible master." The more it berated her, the more exposed, unsettled, and insecure she felt. That's no surprise. Dreaming of bigger and better is one thing. Actually reaching for it can be terrifying. That terror comes from the most ancient part of your brain—the fearful amygdala—and though it means well, it is often misguided and over-reactive. When it worries or warns, you can remind yourself that you do not have to listen. Your thoughts are only thoughts. They may cause you to feel heavy or hopeless, as if you are buried beneath an avalanche or ensnared by unbreakable ties, but they are mere opinions, impressions you've formed, or stories you tell yourself. They do not necessarily reflect reality, and they certainly don't have to be hard-and-fast rules to live by.

I realize I am repeating myself here, but the inner critic is sneaky, savvy, and determined. It knows exactly how to get to us, to manipulate us into falling in line without our even realizing what's happening.

When we believe our fear-based stories to be true, they inhibit us, keeping us stuck in old habits and routines and stunting our progress. Our inner knowing yearns to sing and soar, to stretch and reach. We feel urges and sensations tugging us in a new direction, one that can lead us to greater freedom or joy. Then the inner critic pipes up, terrified and determined to shut us down and keep us safe. We feel stuck in between the two forces, eager and ready to scale the mountain, yet blocked in our ascent. Remarkably, that blockage is the voice of fear and insecurity in our own head. We tell ourselves we "can't disappoint others" or that it's "too late" to try something new. We choose responsibility and obligation over longing. We trudge along, living without feeling fully alive.

What I want you to know is that those burning desires are the domain of your essential self. And though they may grow dim and fade, they can never be fully extinguished. The body registers their presence and neglect by creating tension, heaviness, fatigue, confusion, or despair. The body is trying to get your attention, if only you'd listen.

As for Sierra, shortly after that first call, she and I got to work exploring, naming, and dismantling her fear-based stories one by one, using the tools I will share with you in Chapters Thirteen through Seventeen. We also devised a practical plan of action. Before long, she made a few connections with other musicians via social media, purchased some sound equipment, and started posting video clips of her "playroom performances." Within a few months, she called to tell me that she had booked her first gig at a jazz club near her home. Seeing her on that stage, I felt light and tingly all over, and when I asked her how she felt, she gushed, "There's a feeling of lightness when I'm singing. I feel grounded and connected, but also like I am floating slightly above everything else. When I am truly in the moment, it takes me outside of my everyday reality. It's like an escape, like driving on the open road with the windows down and the wind blowing through my hair, not knowing what's next and not caring. It feels like freedom."

While this may sound like a happy ending, my work with Sierra is ongoing. She still struggles to silence her inner critic, still feels unsure if her "hobby" is a justifiable expense or whether she "has the right" to allocate time to rehearsing and performing when she could be doing her "real job." There is also the challenge of staying positive amidst the inevitable rejections. But through it all, she continues to sing.

Such is the process when we try to break free from painful personal patterns and long-held, deeply ingrained modes of thinking. Progress is rarely linear. We grow in cycles and spurts, moving forward, then back, then forward again. But if we stay the course, somewhere along the way, the inner critic learns to relax. Or at least grow quieter.

You'll find that with practice and experience using the tools in these pages, the intensity and duration of your reactivity and self-doubt will diminish. Lola hasn't disappeared completely—the inner critic never will—but I can tell you that her antics have significantly less impact on me now than they once did. After all, I did write this book, despite her perpetual insults and scare tactics. Luckily, I had the tools to recognize my fear and resist letting it stop me in my tracks. You will also get better at recognizing and managing your fears, not to mention your inner critic. Eventually, when she shows up, you'll welcome her, hear her out, thank her for her concern, then kindly send her on her way.

This is how we begin to change our painful personal patterns.

Would you like a break from your self-critical, repetitive, and exhausting chatter? Do you have any dreams you've been denying? Any passions or plans you've long ignored or relegated to the Land of Someday? Or would you simply like to feel a bit lighter and brighter? What are the thoughts that limit you?

Get ready to disrupt them.

THIRTEEN

The Power of Disruption

 Every time you are tempted to act in the same old way, ask your-self if you want to be a prisoner of the past or a pioneer of the future.

Deepak Chopra

IF YOU'VE EVER TAKEN AN UBER OR EATEN AN IMPOSSIBLE BURGER, you know the power of disrupters—people who look at the established world order and say, "I can improve this." Where others see an impossible challenge, a disrupter sees opportunity. Rather than go with conventional wisdom, they chart their own course. They are thoughtful and intentional about making change. They spot inefficiencies to reform and identify products that could benefit from a refresh. They pay attention to cultural shifts and problems begging to be solved, then set to work shaking things up.

Disrupters do to an industry what I am asking you to do to your own life: Study your personal patterns, spot your weaknesses and painful habits (not in a judgmental way, but with curiosity and compassion), summon the confidence and faith to believe you can change for the better, and get to work blazing a new trail.

If this scares you—or feels like too much work—I urge you to lean into it.

Aiming to disrupt can feel risky, but the rewards can be monumental.

Disrupters weigh the risks against the potential payoff, then plunge ahead. I encourage you to do the same. Whatever potential failure you envision, consider whether it would really be as bad as you fear. The worst that can happen is rarely as bad as we think it is. Plus, the experience of change, and even failure, gives us valuable information for the future while building our resilience at the same time. The alternative is stagnating, running in place, spinning your wheels but going nowhere.

Your inner critic might prefer that, but what about you?

Are you willing to confront the behemoth—to take a critical look at what's working in your life, and what could be better? Might you tap into your inner knowing, summon her support and find the faith in yourself to go in a new direction?

If you've answered, "Hell, yeah!" to any of the above questions, I'd like to invite you to do The Work, my favorite tool for disrupting downward-thinking spirals. The Work is a series of specific questions and turnarounds developed by author and teacher Byron Katie. Katie's book, *Loving What Is: Four Questions That Can Change Your Life*, was assigned reading before my life coach training course had even started, and my reaction to the book was so intense that I almost dropped the class on the spot.

Katie's backstory—she says her awakening came to her one morning on the floor of a halfway house as a cockroach crawled across her foot, and she suddenly grasped the profound difference between reality and our perception of reality—was just too much for me, triggering my most judgmental, skeptical, and dismissive instincts. But the more I practiced Katie's method and experienced the benefits for myself, the more convinced I became of its efficacy and worth. Over the years, I've used The Work to help clients identify and shift a variety of "I suck" thoughts such as: *I am terrible with money. My family doesn't respect me. I lack the experience to apply for that job. I am too old to start dating again. My ideas are not even worth pursuing unless they are guaranteed to be grand/original/impressive/groundbreaking (i.e., perfect).* I also turn to the tool myself whenever I catch myself feeling stressed, anxious, frustrated, insecure, or in any way down on myself.

Katie's method is a step-by-step approach for studying the thoughts in your head, then connecting them with the sensations in your body and your habitual resulting behavior. It is the ultimate expression of *pausing, observing, questioning,* and *reflecting,* and I use it regularly—with myself and my clients—to spot limiting beliefs and loosen their hold, as well as shift perspective and reframe the negative voices that plague so many of us. I don't always stick with Katie's exact script, but whenever I turn to The Work in part or in full, I always find relief.

I can't wait for you to try it!

————

As we've seen, we humans are hardwired for negativity and highly attuned to every grumble and warning from our inner critic. Those worries and concerns may begin as noise in your head, but they eventually manifest in the body, with signals that you can learn to recognize because they will likely be the same, time and time again. If you've been following along with the exercises so far, hopefully you're starting to notice this for yourself. How do fear, uncertainty, embarrassment, hurt feelings, and all the rest show up for you? Recognizing these sensations is your first signal that your personal Lola is on the scene. From there, it's time to turn to The Work. It can be tricky at first, but the more you practice it, the more adept you will become at noticing your painful thoughts and unhelpful habits, then summoning the confidence and faith to implement positive change.

Try the exercise below to get started.

————

Exercise: The Work of Byron Katie

Conjure a thought that upsets you. It might be something from your Greatest Hits list (Chapter Two) or a complaint about others in your life (*My boss doesn't listen to me. My husband is lazy. My parents should be more supportive*). Once you've identified a painful belief, write it down in your notebook, then cycle through the four questions below. Allow yourself time and space here, giving the most meaningful, honest answers you can.

1. Is it true? (Give a simple yes or no, without any explanation. If no, move straight to question 3.)
2. Can you absolutely know that it's true? (Again, give a simple yes or no, no explanation required.)
3. When you are believing the thought, how do you react? What exactly *happens*? Start with physical sensations if you can, but feel free to include emotions and behavior as well. Consider asking yourself some sub-questions, such as: How do you treat other people when you are believing that thought? and How do you treat yourself?
4. If all circumstances remain the same, but you are no longer capable of having this thought, who would you be?

After answering these questions, it is time to explore the turnarounds (which I will explain in more detail below). To do this, take your original stressful thought (e.g., *My mother shouldn't be so judgmental, My husband should be more generous, My son should be more appreciative*) and turn it around to the *opposite* (*My mother should be so judgmental*), the *other* (*I should be more generous toward my husband*), and the *self* (*I should be more appreciative*). From there, find examples from your life of how these new statements are as true as, or truer than, your original thought.

———

If you found that exercise difficult or confusing, please don't worry, as that was merely an introduction. The first few times you do The Work, it can be challenging, which is why I highly recommend reading Katie's book, *Loving What Is*, and/or visiting TheWork.com for additional guidance and practice. Working with a coach who has been trained in the method can be invaluable as well.

For now, I'd like to demonstrate the tool in action by introducing you to Ellie, a client who started a small music studio for children in her hometown. Ellie is an accomplished and creative musician, but she often struggles to execute on her business ideas. She loves everything to do with making and teaching music but has trouble getting excited about doing the promotional part. When she reached out to me for coaching, she was feeling overwhelmed by the marketing aspects of running her studio, as well as the administrative side of things. "Registration, technology, and billing are not my happy place," she told me ruefully. She hired me, she said, to help her "get focused" and "create a new system." She felt "in over her head" and "hopelessly disorganized," terrified that her new business—despite its "amazing potential"—might fail because she "sucked" at staying organized.

Ellie's underlying belief—*I am not organized enough*—is a common one. I have clients with thriving legal practices who lament their "pathetic" approach to billing; successful executives who claim they'd be fired if anyone "knew the truth" about their "nonexistent filing systems"; and women who could give Martha Stewart lessons in homemaking who still fret over their lack of organization at home. Apparently, one can never be too rich, too thin, or too organized.

Let's use Ellie's situation to demonstrate how doing The Work can free someone from the stranglehold of this type of distracting, unhelpful thinking. The following is an edited version of one of our coaching sessions, where I guided Ellie through Katie's questions.

What are you believing to be true in this situation? What is the limiting belief or painful thought?
I should be more organized and get more done.

Is it true?
Yes.

Can you absolutely know that it is true?
No.

How do you react, what happens, when you believe that thought?
I feel burdened, heavy, and defeated. I feel hopeless and incapable of pressing forward. Believing that I should be more organized fills me with dread and guilt. It makes me doubt myself and my ability to run this new business. It also makes me feel frantic—my heart races, my jaw locks, my whole body tenses. I get hyperfocused on "getting stuff done," but at the same time, I get paralyzed. I don't know where to start. I start on one thing, then switch to something else, and something else. It becomes a vicious cycle. Everything gets messier!

How do you treat others when you are actively believing that thought?
Badly. I get impatient and occasionally lose my temper. I take my frustrations out on my children and husband as if their needs are additional burdens I can't quite handle. When I get frenetic and launch into too many things, this makes me and my family perpetually late. Then, I blame everyone else for the lateness. I also neglect my husband. He sends me emails throughout the day—articles he thinks I will appreciate, questions about upcoming plans, thoughtful notes for no reason—and rather than appreciate that he is thinking about me, I treat his messages like an annoying interruption.

How do you treat yourself?
Horribly! I judge myself harshly for my lack of organization, my impa-

tience with my children, and my inattention to my husband. Oddly, I also beat myself up for not being more "calm and relaxed." I begin to doubt my abilities and my future. How can I be a creative, inspiring teacher for other people's children when this is how I am in my own life?

If your circumstances were exactly the same and your life were exactly as it is now, but you were no longer capable of thinking *I should be more organized and get more done*, who would you be?
I'd be far more relaxed! Happier and more patient with myself and everyone else. I'd be more at ease, more go-with-the-flow. Just thinking about it, I feel less tense and panicky. I'd be more loving to my family. I feel I could probably be more productive, too.

These questions helped Ellie see how her "I should be more organized and get more done" story impacted her energy, her enthusiasm for her work, her productivity, and her interactions with her family and clients. Taking the time to pause and observe the tension and stress she was experiencing, then pondering and answering the questions, allowed Ellie to comprehend—and feel— how her perpetual dissatisfaction and discomfort had as much to do with her thinking as with her lack of organization. With the final question, she was able to experience the freedom of letting that go and seeing for herself what her life and career might look and feel like if she simply removed the thinking.

The Turnarounds

If Byron Katie's initial questions help loosen the grip of limiting beliefs, the turnarounds are what blaze new neural pathways. By taking our original negative thought (e.g., *I should be more organized*), then turning it around three different ways—to the *opposite*, to the *other*, and to the *self*—we uncover the evidence our brain needs to form new modes of thinking. When doing the turnarounds with my clients, I start by asking them to turn the original thought into its opposite. In Ellie's case, *I should be more organized* became *I am organized enough, and I get enough done*. From there, I asked her to provide three pieces of evidence to support this new, alternative thought. Ellie told me that (1) she usually does complete her daily tasks and responsibilities (at least the truly important ones); (2) her business is growing, largely due to her solo efforts; and (3) she always pays her bills in full and on time, while taking sufficient (if not perfect) care of her family and household.

As she reported her evidence, Ellie's tone grew less damning and more confident. Her painful thought about her lack of organization had been so absolute, but citing examples of the opposite began to reveal some cracks. This is the magic of questioning our limiting beliefs: they rarely hold up when we confront them directly.

The other turnarounds are, in my opinion, much trickier to describe, so please bear with me here.

With the second turnaround, we are asked to turn the original thought to the other, which essentially asks us to switch the subjects in our thought sentences. (For example, the thought *Jenny should be more affectionate toward me* turns around to *I should be more affectionate toward Jenny*.) In situations where the original painful thought is about another person—like a spouse, child, or colleague—reversing subjects is fairly straightforward. Using this turnaround when a thought is about oneself—whether an "I suck" thought or otherwise —is a bit tougher but can really open you up to new and creative ways of looking at the world.

In Ellie's case, her turnaround to the other involved a personification of "organized," so that *I should be more organized* became *Organized should be more me*. (I told you this is hard to describe!) When I asked her for three examples of how this turnaround might be just as true as the original thought (if not truer), Ellie laughed, and I could feel the tension and self-recrimination leave her body.

"Wow," she said. "Just, wow!"

"What's happening?" I asked her.

"I can't believe I never thought about this before. 'Organized' is closed, whereas I am more creative. 'Organized' is obsessive, whereas I am more relaxed and open-minded. 'Organized' is fixed and rigid, but I am nimble and flexible. The more I think about it, the more I like myself the way I am, and my music and this new business reflect that. My studio is a relaxed and inviting place, the kids don't have to worry about being perfect or hitting every note just right. It's a place to explore, take risks, and get inspired. I encourage the students to be spontaneous, to improvise and experiment. There is no place for 'organized' in all of that!"

I asked Ellie to sit with that for a moment and let it sink in. Then we moved on to the third and final turnaround—to the self. Ellie turned *I should be more organized* into *I should be more myself*. Again, she laughed as soon as she said it. (Laughter, by the way, is inner-knowing gold, an indication that we've hit on something essential and true.) When I asked why she was laughing, she told me she could not believe how much full-body relief this was giving her.

Sticking with the script, I asked her for three examples to support her new *I should be more myself* thought.

Here, Ellie sounded solid and confident as she declared, "I like myself the way I am and don't need to change. Just by being me, I have created a beautiful life. I have remained true to my artistic passion. I have just started a new business, and it is already growing. I manage to get lots of things done in a mostly organized way, but with flexibility and openness. Do I want the business to thrive? Of course, I do. But the business is me being me, doing what I do best. And when I try to be rigid, uptight, and more organized, I am not at my best."

As Ellie and countless others have discovered, doing The Work is an incredibly effective method for letting go (or at least easing the grip) of painful thoughts and patterns, a gateway to discovering how we might feel and what we might do once we liberate ourselves from our self-imposed limitations. And if this all feels confusing or under-whelming to you, that's okay. My intention here is to introduce you to Katie's method and show how it can help to disrupt negative thinking. But please understand that reading *about* The Work is about as effective as reading a manual on bicep curls. It is informative and even points you in the right direction, but you won't reap any benefits until you do the exercises yourself. Repeatedly.

As for Ellie, last we spoke, she was in a much better place, both emotionally and financially. She has continued doing what she loves, but with more confidence, excitement, and joy. From what I hear, young families all over her community are better for it.

FOURTEEN

I Have Her Still

 It's not what you look at that matters; it's what you see.

Henry David Thoreau

RECENTLY, I WAS OUT IN THE WOODS WITH MY DOG, RIVER, relishing the spring sunshine and feeling deeply grateful that, after a morning of back-to-back clients, I'd carved out the time to do my favorite hike. Before long, however, I found myself lost in thought, reliving a series of events from my thirties, when I was still reeling from my mother's death, and ambivalent about which direction to go in my life.

As I walked, familiar phrases bubbled up to the surface. *If I had known then what I know now, I would have… Maybe if I had chosen a different practice area… Maybe if my mother hadn't died….*

I knew exactly where this was going, since my mind had wandered here many times before. The question was why, after all these years, on this beautiful day, was I flailing in a sea of regret when everything in the here and now was just as I wanted it to be? Or, at least, pretty damn close!

Instinctively, I paused and observed my thinking. Then it hit me.

Earlier that day, I'd gotten an email from my former law firm. They were looking to hire more associates and offering financial incentives to alumni who sent them any referrals. Given how many young lawyers I coach, I gave the email serious consideration, wondering if I knew anyone right for the firm. What I hadn't realized, however, was the extent to which the message unearthed all my old stories about who I was "supposed" to be and what I was "meant" to accomplish: legal superstardom, not midday hikes between coaching clients and after-school pickups.

The story I was telling myself is that I'd copped out when the going got tough—that rather than staying the course and killing it in my career, I took the "easy way out"—that is, marriage and motherhood. The story was that I could have tried harder to "have it all," but that instead, I'd failed. The story was that I "sucked."

As I hiked along, I noticed a tightness in my chest and a bitterness in my throat, a tinge of nausea in my belly and a sense of weakness in my limbs. I wanted to cry or throw up or scream. I felt sick and angry all over again about the choices I had made at a time when it felt as if I had no choices—because my mother had died. *If she'd lived, I would have gotten the guidance I needed. If she'd lived, I would have had help with my daughter. If she'd lived, I would have felt stronger and more confident about my decisions, instead of making them from a weak and vulnerable place. If she'd lived, everything would have been different. Easier. Better.* My thoughts continued to spiral until I came to what seemed like an inevitable conclusion: *I'd been cheated.*

Those three little words stopped me in my tracks. Suddenly, I was back in the present, noticing the way River was trotting happily up the trail, his tail wagging and his head held high. I noticed the breeze in the pine trees and the birdsong around me.

Where had I gone? Why had I let myself travel to such a dark place in the midst of all this beauty? What was the painful story that had swept me away?

I was cheated.

This line felt new. Suddenly, I realized that I had been holding on to this belief without awareness, believing it so deeply and completely that it had never occurred to me to name it, much less question it. But that's what disrupting unhealthy patterns requires: paying attention and investigating anything and everything that feels painful or oppressive.

As I often do with my clients mired in stressful thinking habits, I turned to The Work to probe more deeply beneath my "I was cheated" story. This is how it went:

I was cheated.

Is it true?
Yes.

Could I absolutely know it was true?
Ummm ….

It was very tempting to say yes, to insist to myself that I was cheated by my mother's early death at age fifty-six, especially after I had already lost my father. But how could I "absolutely" know that? How can we "absolutely" know anything? Perhaps I needed to lose her in that way, at that time, to arrive where I was now. As I paused and questioned my belief, I almost instantly began to feel a slight loosening in the chest, a subtle opening in my throat.

When I believe I was cheated, what happens? How do I react?
I feel like a victim, and I want to lash out at the people I love. I get sad or feel sick, sullen, and bitter. Sometimes I even begrudge everyone else their good fortune for still having their mother—or, luckier still, both parents—when I've had to suffer through being alone for so long.

At that, I pause again, because the word "alone" jumps out at me. It signals another painful story I choose to dismantle on the spot. I am far from alone. I have Rob and the kids, my brother, my in-laws, and a huge extended family. I have more friends than I can count and a whole community I love and cherish. And then there's River, right by my side. I am most definitely not alone.

I continue with the inquiry.

When I believe that I was cheated, how do I treat others?

I feign toughness and push them away. I disconnect, go inward, maybe even go off to sulk somewhere. I make *myself alone.*

Which brings me to the fourth question:

Who would I be without my "I was cheated" story?

Well, I would be a girl who misses her mom but isn't so angry. I would feel lighter and more at ease. I would feel less bitterness and resentment toward others and more appreciative of everything I do have. I'd be less of a victim and more empowered, less of a sullen child, and more gracious, connected, compassionate, and proud.

I breathe that in, feeling the shift to this brighter, stronger, more peaceful state. I linger there, enjoying the transition, and then I move on to the next stage of The Work, the turnarounds.

What is the opposite of "I was cheated"?

I was blessed. I am *blessed.*

What are three examples of how the story "I am blessed" is just as true, if not truer, than "I was cheated"?

Here, my nausea subsides, my chest breaks open, the breath I didn't know I was holding whooshes free, and my face breaks into that wide "the answer was with me all along" smile.

My examples:
I had the greatest mother a girl could ask for.
I had her until I was almost thirty.
I have her still.

Peace and gratitude wash over me, tears flood my eyes, and all the pain and sorrow subside.

I have her still.

I stay with that, basking in the relief it brings, taking deep breaths and looking up at the impossibly blue sky. I feel so much better that I stop the exercise there, skipping the other two turn-arounds. Instead, I marvel at the way the sun is streaming through the trees, as if my mother is up there smiling at me, waiting for me to notice. I smile back, resting in the warmth and comfort that has replaced the bitterness of a few moments earlier. I think about all the ways my mother lives on in me and in my children, in my brother and his new baby. I think of all the lessons she instilled that I continue to draw from: to find ways to laugh every day, even through difficulty; to celebrate the beauty and creativity in others; and to equate motherhood with acceptance and devotion, unwavering support, and heaps of affection. Most of all, I think of how I feel her unconditional love to this day.

FIFTEEN

Let It R.A.I.N

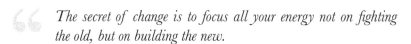

The secret of change is to focus all your energy not on fighting the old, but on building the new.

Socrates

Now that we've gotten this far, I want to acknowledge that it's not always easy to fight dark, pessimistic feelings or tune out the inner critic. Admittedly, there's a lot to feel discouraged about in this world: brutal wars, pandemics, dysfunctional governments, divisive politics, systemic injustice, and, of course, climate change. Closer to home, in the past few years, I've lost two very close friends to cancer, and two more are battling their way through. Sometimes I also feel as if I am "losing" my children, even as they sit beside me at the kitchen table. They are taller than I am now, and their chubby, squeezable limbs have given way to longer, less huggable teenage bodies. I know they still love me, but these days, they are more likely to be annoyed by than enamored with me, their once constant smiles mostly replaced by eye-rolling. This, of course, is as it should be. But that doesn't mean it hurts any less. Despite all I've learned as a coach, in my lower moments I'm sometimes tempted to abandon my training and adopt Lola's more negative worldview. That's when I know it's time to turn to another one of my favorite tools. It's called R.A.I.N., which stands for *recognize*, *allow*, *investigate*, *nurture*. I first learned this exercise from Tara Brach, whom we encountered earlier. R.A.I.N takes any fear-based, narrow, or negative perspective and helps us broaden our way of thinking so we can identify, name, and detach from painful thoughts and move toward a more lighthearted place of possibility.

As you explore this tool, you may notice that parts of it can feel similar to doing The Work, since both methods encourage acknowledging and pushing back against painful thoughts, then allowing for alternative possibilities. You will also recognize other concepts I've talked a lot about, such as *pausing*, *observing*, *questioning*, *clarifying*, *confronting*, and *negativity bias*. That repetition is by design. None of these tools are meant to be one-and-done. To go from basic survival mode to a more evolved state of thriving, you'll need to practice these strategies repeatedly, discovering which one (or two or three) resonate and work best for you.

As for R.A.I.N., I suggest trying it whenever you notice yourself feeling discouraged, self-doubting, or down in any way. Here's how it works.

Start with the *R* in this acronym, which stands for *recognize*. As you know, the first step to solving any problem is awareness. That's why I place so much emphasis on *pausing*, *observing*, *questioning*, and *reflecting*. That's how you begin to map out your personal, painful habits. The more you practice POQR—the more you collect your data, tune in to your body, and connect the dots between your thoughts and their impact—the more familiar you become with your own physical and emotional patterns. That makes it much easier to catch yourself slipping into a state of stress or insecurity—to recognize it—then remind yourself to get curious and investigate what happens in your body and mind when you are in a charged place. Note how that feeling shows itself in your fists or throat, your energy level, or your reactions to others. Then pause again, take a deep breath, and go inward. The only thing to do here is to *recognize* and breathe, to get out of mindless autopilot, and intentionally check in with your present experience.

The second letter, *A*, for *allow*, is a reminder to make space for whatever you are experiencing, to give your sensations and thoughts the time, opportunity, and permission to just be. Allowing is a moment of pure stillness in which you merely sit with your feelings immediately after recognizing you've been triggered. This step may sound simple, but it sure as hell isn't easy. That's because very few of us spend time just *being* or *allowing* our experience. We want to avoid or fix, run, hide, fight back, numb, distract, or do anything but stay present. This part of R.A.I.N. requires us to let go of those unhelpful strategies and simply let the feelings exist. After all, our feelings show up for a reason, and they need to be felt. As uncomfortable as it is to sit with unpleasant feelings—be they physical or emotional—denying those feelings or shoving them down is unlikely to help. In the words of neuroanatomist and author Jill Bolte Taylor, "[We] are programmed to feel our emotions, and any attempt we may make to bypass or ignore what we are feeling may have the power to derail our mental health."[13] Or to paraphrase Carl Jung, *what we resist tends to persist.* By contrast, sitting with intense or difficult feelings helps them go from a boil to a simmer, which makes more clearheaded, capable responses possible.

At first, I was tempted to skip the *allowing* step; as you've probably gathered by now, I'm a person of action. Now, it's my favorite part of R.A.I.N. Even if I take just a minute to sit and breathe and allow my feelings, these rare moments of *being* are a necessary antidote to all the *doing*. Sitting with painful feelings teaches us that we can survive them and that merely being uncomfortable does not kill us but may ultimately leave us stronger and more capable. Make it a habit and, like me, you'll learn to relish the experience of letting whatever is happening happen, knowing there is nothing to do and nothing to fix, at least for a moment.

Before we go on to explore the *I* of R.A.I.N., I want to encourage you, once again, to consider adopting a meditation practice, even if you start with just five or ten minutes per session. *Recognizing* and *allowing* your thoughts, feelings, and emotions can only be enhanced by the practice. That is because the essence of meditation is sitting and breathing while you try to stay present and focused, whether on the breath, some other sensation, or a mantra. But notice I said *try*. Even the most seasoned meditators always return to the activity of thinking. Many beginners believe this makes them bad at meditation, but I assure you, the trying, faltering, and trying again *is the whole point*. Meditation encourages us to accept and be with the moment as is—intrusive thoughts and all—but also to keep letting go and returning to the breath. In that way, it teaches us to notice when we've gotten lost in our thoughts, then gently reminds us to release them. In the process, we are encouraged to suspend judgment, to observe our thoughts without getting swept away by them, to let them come and let them go—and again, to return to the breath.

Can you see why I am such a fan? This practice of sitting with discomfort, of noticing your thoughts—critical and otherwise—and letting them go, then *guiding* yourself to a calmer place, is fundamental to taming your inner critic. And the more you practice on the cushion (or floor, or chair, or wherever you choose to meditate), the more readily you will do the same thing in your daily life. Everything I've been encouraging you to do, from thinking twice to collecting your data, from noticing your body's signals to cultivating the awareness required to pull out your tools in the first place, well…*all* of these crucial skills can be abetted by regular mediation.

Which brings me to the third letter in R.A.I.N.—*I* for *investigate*. In this step, after you've spent some time *allowing*, you dig deeper, getting curious about what you are experiencing and asking questions. A few things you might ask yourself at this stage: *Why am I suddenly stressed or tense or shaking with fear? Why is my stomach in knots? What exactly is the story I am telling myself? What am I believing to be true at this moment?*

This is your opportunity to implement much of what we've been discussing. First, notice if a particular person or situation has set you off. Then zero in on what it is you are thinking about. Is it an email from the boss that says "Please come see me" that is causing you to panic? Or is it your interpretation of what the email might mean? If you believe you are about to be reprimanded or critiqued, your physical and emotional response will be tense, defensive, or even hostile. In contrast, if you remind yourself that the truth is likely less threatening (think: "She probably has a question and doesn't have time to put it in writing"), you will pop into her office with a more open and willing frame of mind. Once you start questioning, you may discover that even stories that feel absolutely true may not be; there may be evidence that supports another story.

Stick with your investigation until you come to something that feels like a nugget of truth. You'll know you're there when you experience a settled feeling, smile a knowing smile, or move from discomfort to a feeling of release and calm.

From there you can pause again, scan through your life, and gauge how this particular strain of negative thinking has affected you. Whatever story you identify—*No one respects me; I am not smart enough; I've always had to do everything twice as well as everyone else*—reflect on how it might be affecting your career, your behavior, or your relationships. Think about whether it has been helping you or not. How does it impact your happiness?

As part of your self-investigation, search your history. Locate and observe your defensive patterns and self-deprecating thoughts. Consider how much time you've lost or how much suffering you've experienced at the hands of your own troublesome thinking. How would you like to feel instead?

The value here, in my experience, is in developing an appreciation for how much of our pain and suffering is self-imposed. This isn't so you can berate yourself further or wallow in regret about it, but so you can stop doing it. As we've explored, all too often, we experience an added level of suffering, over and above any painful situation, that comes from our thinking. For those of us who are self-critical, it's easy to layer some form of self-blame—*I should have known better!*—on top of an already difficult situation. Buddhists call this "the second arrow" because the pain doesn't just come from what is happening to you (the first arrow), but from your own self-imposed harsh judgment. My hope is that you see this for what it is —unnecessary and unhelpful—and extend yourself some compassion instead. What might you tell a friend going through similar difficulties? Would you attack him for his inability to buck up and get on with life, or might you offer some kindness instead?

This brings us to the final letter of R.A.I.N.— *N* for *nurture*. This is where R.A.I.N. truly differs from some of the other techniques in this book. R.A.I.N. is ultimately a tool of self-compassion, where you learn to identify your deepest needs and find a way to get those needs met.

The idea is to soothe yourself, giving yourself nurturing in painful moments of doubt. You can mentally call on someone benevolent and kind, someone you love and trust, for comfort and reassurance. This can be your wise inner knowing or someone else in your life—living or dead, known to you or a public figure—who you trust to give you solace. It can even be a beloved pet. As you do this, Tara Brach suggests putting your hand on your heart to lock in the sensation of nurturing care. This gesture felt awkward to me at first, but then I read about some research by Kristin Neff, PhD, associate professor of educational psychology at the University of Texas at Austin, on the power of compassionate physical gestures.[14] Neff is a pioneer in the field of self-compassion research, and she has found that physical touch reduces cortisol, a stress hormone, and releases oxytocin, a neurochemical often referred to as the "love drug," which is also triggered when mothers nurse their babies. Higher levels of oxytocin, Neff states, "strongly increase feelings of trust, calm, safety, generosity, and connectedness," and she invites us, just like Brach, to use soothing forms of physical touch on ourselves, whether stroking our own face or gently rocking our body to calm ourselves when we feel tense, insecure, or self-critical.[15]

No wonder when an infant cries, we are quick to scoop them into our arms and hold them in close. If a friend is struggling, we offer a hand to hold or a shoulder to cry on, maybe even a hug. We know the healing power of physical touch instinctively, so why not offer it to ourselves?

Despite my initial awkwardness, when I arrive at this stage of R.A.I.N. nowadays, I close my eyes, wrap my arms around myself, and picture my mom. I imagine her stroking my hair or rubbing my back, offering heavily accented words of comfort. In these moments, I sink into that old sensation of safety and warmth that comes from knowing, at the deepest level, that I am loved no matter what. The situation may suck, but I do not. Whatever I have done wrong or have failed to accomplish, whatever mistakes I have made or disappointment I have caused—it's all okay. I may have some work to do to repair the situation, but the misstep, whatever it is, does not define me. "You can work on that if you want to," I imagine my mother saying, "but I love you just the way you are."

———

Exercise: Exploring R.A.I.N

Recognizing and undoing toxic patterns is crucial to living well, and in my experience, R.A.I.N. always delivers that self-knowledge. To practice, draw up some of your own self-judgments and perseverations, but this time, don't give them any power. Instead: *Recognize* what is going on. *Allow* the experience to be there, as it is. *Investigate* with interest and care. *Nurture* yourself with self-compassion. You can practice this on your own, as a form of meditation, or you can summon the tool whenever you notice yourself sliding into negativity of any kind. To help you get started, please visit TaraBrach.com/meditation-practice-rain/ and allow Tara Brach to walk you through it.

———

SIXTEEN

Get Playful

 People tend to forget that play is serious.

David Hockney

By now, you are well equipped to dismantle your most limiting stories, engage on a whole new level with your inner critic, and get some relief. You know when to pause and get curious, to ask questions and turn your negativity around.

Next, I want to introduce some more playful approaches to challenging the bully in your head, and even befriending her. Some of these are shortcuts to exposing your inner critic and generating greater awareness, and some are silly, lighthearted approaches to silencing her on the spot. After all, most of us are pressed for time, and pretty much all of us could use a bit more play in our life—a reason to take our insecurities and self-criticism less seriously. And trust me, when you practice bringing levity and humor to painful "I suck" moments, you take away some of the sting of self-doubt. Learning to laugh at yourself will help lighten your mood and restore your energy. The less bogged down you feel by your own mental muck, the more accustomed you'll get to feeling freer and better, which will help you pick up on any hint of internal fear or stress before they take a toll.

Cross-Examining the Witness

One of my favorite fun tools for defanging the inner critic is something I call Cross-Examining the Witness. (It's the lawyer in me; I can't help it.) Imagine a scenario where you've made a mistake or done something careless. What happens? If you're anything like me, your inner critic launches into a rant—*You're stupid and irresponsible and can't do anything right!*—attacking your judgment and lashing you with insults. Should you find yourself in the throes of such negative self-talk, rather than taking the abuse, try summoning your best TV trial lawyer impersonation and put your inner critic on the witness stand instead. Picture yourself standing tall and proud, armed with conviction, your team of colleagues sitting at the table behind you. Imagine a packed courtroom, everyone eager to hear you make a compelling and winning case. Then picture your inner critic sitting across from you, having just been sworn in, shaky and weak with fear. She isn't used to being challenged, isn't used to dealing with you in this bold new role. You've never questioned her before, and she suddenly realizes her insults are unlikely to hold up under interrogation.

You sense her vulnerability, and it emboldens you.

"Inner critic," you begin. "Is it true that I am stupid?"

"Yes…" she attempts.

"Allow me to remind you that you are under oath," you press. "Is it true that I am stupid?"

"No," she says meekly.

"Is it true that I am irresponsible?" you continue.

"No," she whispers.

"I can't hear you. Please repeat your answer."

"No!" she admits. (You're starting to enjoy yourself now.)

The idea here is not to get into an argument with your inner critic. It's more about poking holes in her story and, to take the lawyer analogy further, creating some reasonable doubt. According to your inner critic's testimony, you "suck." Whether that's because you are "a spineless, ineffective loser who is never going to get ahead" or "a terrible mother" for having snapped at your child and made her cry, you don't need to contradict the painful story in its entirety or "prove" the inner critic wrong. In these acute moments of pain, all you need is to create enough space between the extremes to find some comfort and proceed with greater ease, and the best way to do that is to find evidence. After cross-examining your inner critic, you'll want to build an alternative story, listing examples that weaken her case against you. Scan through your experience for proof that you are not "stupid and irresponsible and can't do anything right." Remind your inner critic, and yourself, of the many right things you've done in your life, the many ways you are capable.

If you are especially self-doubting or critical, consider creating a physical file documenting the evidence of your wins. Essentially, this Win File is a collection, whether mental, digital or physical, of your successes and smart choices—a place to list your accomplishments as well as any personal qualities you appreciate, or feel are worth celebrating.

One client, Jason, a fortysomething actor-turned-lawyer with a rather relentless inner critic he has dubbed Boss Baby, tried the Win File tool with good results. In our early sessions, he told me that Boss Baby's favorite bedtime story featured Jason as a hapless under-achiever who "wasted too many good years" pursing his passion for acting, only to realize it was "never going anywhere" and that he needed to "wake up, get serious, and get a real job." All these years later, even with his law career going strong, Jason told me that he still struggled to reconcile his earlier choices to pursue acting. Boss Baby had him convinced he "sucked" because he "should have been further along," both professionally and financially. This critical voice was especially likely to be triggered when Jason pondered splurging on a vacation or making a large purchase, or when something happened at work that made him "feel his age" compared with his younger colleagues. I suggested that the next time that happened, he focus on creating a Win File of all the things he was proud of. When he shared his list with me, a Google doc titled "Jason's Wins, Big,

Small, and In No Particular Order," I couldn't help but smile. What started almost like a résumé, listing schools attended and jobs secured, expanded to include things like settling his debts and being a trusted friend, a fun uncle, a dependable team-player, and "not an asshole."

Jason told me that when he looks at his Win File, it reminds him of his abilities, but also the larger story of who he is ("a whole person, greater than the sum of my flaws"), which helps him feel more confident. My guess is, if you adopt the practice yourself, you will too.

––––––

Exercise: Cross-Examine the Witness

Go ahead and pretend to be a TV lawyer. Revisit your Greatest Hits list or identify any "I suck" thoughts you can think of. Then put your inner critic on the witness stand and do your best trial lawyer impersonation. Write a short script for yourself and act it out. Be as theatrical as you like. Be sure to include as much evidence as possible to support your case—including your own personal Win File—and expose your inner critic for the fraud she is.

––––––

The Hokey Pokey

Another playful and easy way to short-circuit habitual negative thinking is to move your body; the goal is to disrupt static thinking with active movement. Whenever you find yourself slipping down a negativity slide, get moving instead. Do some jumping jacks or burpees. Go for a walk. Spin around in circles or stand on your head. Put your left hand in, put your left hand out, put your left hand in, and shake it all about. Whatever you do, don't just stand there. Do something to physically shake off the negativity and redirect yourself.

My personal favorite way of stopping a negativity spiral is to take a walk—ideally in the woods. Immersing yourself in nature is one of the best ways I know to silence the mental prattle, to recharge and gain a wider perspective. There is a lot of science behind this, with a growing body of research establishing an undeniable link between time spent in nature—whether parks, forests, beaches, or backyards—and enhanced well-being. If you are interested, I recommend reading *The Nature Fix: Why Nature Makes Us Happier, Healthier, and More Creative* by Florence Williams. Or you can just get out there and see for yourself.

If you live in a city or otherwise have limited access to open spaces, please know that even small doses of nature can help. Try to seek out green spaces, contribute to a community garden, stroll down a tree-lined street, watch the sunrise, or consider adding some plants to your home or office. Find some way to connect with the natural world so that you, too, can reap the mood-boosting, stress-reducing power and benefits.

Then again, nature isn't the only way to shake things up. Consider visiting an art exhibit, seeing a show, taking a day trip to a new town, or experimenting with a new recipe. Almost any change of scenery or routine can do the trick. Whenever clients complain of feeling bored, sapped of creativity or overly burdened by routine, I suggest the same.

For me, going elsewhere has always been a lure. Just before my twenty-first birthday, while most of my friends seemed thrilled to toss their fake IDs, I suddenly found myself wanting more. The yearning came on instantaneously as if I had been bitten by something. And maybe I had: the travel bug! With my big birthday approaching, it hit me that by the time my mother was my age, she had owned and sold a business, served in the Israeli army, and immigrated to the United States, where she knew no one, to create a whole new life.

In contrast, all I'd done was excel at school and party a bit on the side.

I remember having a vision of myself, decades older, a gray-haired grandmother rocking in a chair by a fireplace. I imagined grandchildren at my feet clamoring for stories from my life, and me realizing I had nothing to share. I had been so attached to my straight and narrow path toward ultimate success, so consumed by getting where I needed to go in life, that I'd forgotten to *live*.

Shortly after, I began my junior year semester abroad in Tel Aviv. Every day presented opportunities for adventure, whether it was exploring the city on a moped, camping out under the stars at the edge of the Dead Sea, or sharing a hookah in a tent with a Bedouin. The experience so whetted my appetite for adventure that I graduated college a semester early and deferred law school for a year so I could travel more. Suddenly I had a new goal: accumulating stories and exploring new terrain.

And accumulate I did. I backpacked through Egypt and Jordan, visited friends in Rome and Venice, and wandered for a month through Vietnam, negotiating my way across cities on the tightest budget. Everywhere I went, I was wide-eyed and eager, engaged, curious, and fully present. At times it was challenging and even terrifying, but the pull to adventure was undeniable, fueled by a mysterious force within I can only describe as freedom. I *felt* free—from pressure, from my past, and even from my future, with no agenda and no burdens.

I've never forgotten that time. And though I can no longer instantly decide to cross continents when I feel the urge to run away, I do pause and breathe, then try to get adventurous closer to home. For instance, when my son was five, we played tourist in our hometown of New York City, exploring a new neighborhood one afternoon each week. Alphabet City in the far East Village was up first, then a walk across the Brooklyn Bridge, a wander through Chinatown, then Dumbo in Brooklyn, the Empire State Building, the Flatiron District, the Guggenheim, and so on.

With each mini-vacation, I felt the same excitement, escape, and inspiration as I had on those long-ago journeys abroad. Well... maybe not *exactly* the same, but surprisingly close to it!

Putting yourself somewhere different, switching up the scenery, even if that means walking a different route with the dog or driving to work a different way, can jump-start your thinking. That's a good thing, because breaking up with old habits requires an active, engaged mind.

Incidentally, taking up a new hobby or learning a new skill can offer many of the same benefits. When you do anything new, whether learning to play the piano or how to ski, it's essential to be present and focused rather than on autopilot. The opportunity to be a novice can, of course, get frustrating, but only if you tell yourself that you "should" be more skilled or that your fumbling is embarrassing. There's another option: afford yourself the space to try and fail, and, more often than not, you'll emerge feeling exhilarated and proud.

––––––

Exercise: Turn Yourself Around

Identify three possible options for turning yourself around in the event of an inner critic onslaught. Whether it's doing the actual hokey pokey or taking a walk, breaking out your watercolors or skydiving, booking a local Airbnb or taking a trip across the world, name your strategies. Write them down in your notebook. Then, the next time an opportunity to disrupt a negativity spiral arises, take it.

––––––

Phone a Friend

If you've ever watched *Who Wants to Be A Millionaire*, you know exactly what I mean by "Phone a Friend." If you're not familiar with the show, that's okay. Just know it was a game show in which contestants had to answer a series of increasingly difficult multiple-choice questions to win a cash prize. If a contestant was stumped, they had the option to use a variety of lifelines, one of which allowed them to call a friend to see if they could provide the answer.

I haven't watched the show in over twenty years, but Phone a Friend has always stuck with me. Now I use it as a coaching tool. Essentially, it's just a playful way of reminding my hard-working, high-achieving clients that they don't always have to do everything themselves, and they don't always have to have all the answers. They are allowed to falter or feel unsure, and when they do, reaching out to a friend will likely serve them far better than their painful "I suck" thinking.

Beyond taming your inner critic or otherwise picking yourself up when you're feeling down, enlisting the support of others can help keep you accountable and keep you on track when it comes to pursuing goals. Whether you want to stick with an exercise routine, give up alcohol, or adopt a meditation practice, involving a friend in the effort can make difficult challenges significantly more fun and might ultimately make all the difference.

Seeking out friends for support may seem too obvious a strategy to mention, but personally, I often need the reminder. I lean heavily in the direction of self-reliance. *Pausing, observing, questioning,* and *reflecting* feel very natural to me. Ditto for digging deep, pinpointing problems, and crafting solutions. Asking for help, however, does not come as easily. Thanks to this work, I am getting better at it.

I speak to my own coach regularly and always appreciate the gift of those hours, the comfort of letting everything out and putting myself into her competent hands. But the support I truly relish comes from family and friends. I've taken to scheduling calls with cousins and cross-country friends as if they were appointments with clients. Sometimes we just catch up; other times we hash over something specific. I make it a point to have regular dinner dates with my crew from high school, as well as hikes, coffee dates, and dinner plans with newer friends closer to home. My former law firm colleagues were by far the best part of the job—having colleagues you can confide in is one of the greatest outlets for easing the stress of work—and we continue to support one another all these years later. When there is something to cry about or something to celebrate, reaching out to others may not be instinctive, but it always delivers.

Favorite Things

Before we move on to more serious matters, I'd like to introduce you to one more game. It is called Favorite Things, and while it isn't necessarily a tool to pull out in the middle of an inner critic attack (though it could be!), it is the kind of daily practice that can diminish the frequency of those attacks to begin with.

I first created the game back when my children were little and bedtime was still an important ritual in my house. After books and cuddles, and before saying good night, everyone would think back on five favorite things that had happened that day. It might be kick-ball at recess, an after-school playdate in Central Park, or the ice cream cones we stopped for on the way home. Someone—usually Layla—always ended the whole thing by shouting "Pillows!" and burrowing into a soft pile nearby, or attempting to start a pillow fight, depending on the night. Either way, everyone went to bed pretty smiley.

Favorite Things began after I attended a lecture by Tal Ben-Shahar, PhD, Harvard professor and bestselling author of many books, including *Happier: Learn the Secrets to Daily Joy and Lasting Fulfillment*. The lecture had been my introduction to the world of positive psychology and the benefits of practicing gratitude, and it could not have come at a better time. Still reeling from the loss of my mother, I found deep relief and unexpected comfort in the notion that simple gratitude could alleviate such tremendous pain. When Ben-Shahar talked about the benefits of focusing on the positive just before bed and told us that he did so with his young son every night, I was inspired to do the same.

In the years since, as I've delved deeper into the research, my gratitude practice has evolved. Study after study has shown that people who consistently practice gratitude are more optimistic, enthusiastic, energetic, and joyful.[16] They also tend to be more emotionally intelligent and apt to forgive, as well as less depressed, anxious, and lonely.[17] They sleep better and generally feel more socially connected, more trusting, and better able to relate to others.[18] The best thing about it is that people aren't happy because they already have it good; they feel happy because they choose to be grateful.

In short, practicing gratitude is one of the most beneficial things you can do for yourself, as well as one of the simplest. Consider adopting your own version of Favorite Things with your family or find a gratitude buddy you can exchange texts with each day. Or just set aside a few minutes to jot down, or at least think about, the parts of your life you appreciate—especially the everyday positives we tend to overlook. I encourage people to be very specific, to scan the day and take note of that perfect cup of coffee or an unexpected kindness from a colleague. You might even express gratitude for simple yet essential things like a hot shower or sufficient food in your pantry, or the absence of something (like pain in your back or illness), or the role of cherished people in your life, past or present.

Right now, for me, I am feeling grateful for a gentle knock on my office door from Summer, my younger daughter. She is "making a stress ball for Daddy" and needs my help shoving fistfuls of sand into a balloon, the most adorable interruption of the day so far.

SEVENTEEN

Love the One You're With

 If your compassion does not include yourself, it is incomplete.

Jack Kornfield

By now, I hope one thing is very clear: YOU DO *NOT* SUCK. I want you to know and love and value yourself. I want you to accept, appreciate, and care for yourself, to celebrate your strengths, forgive your weaknesses, and warmly embrace the whole of who you are. Self-love is a superpower, though one that takes conscious effort to develop. All the tools in this chapter are designed to get you there.

Self-Compassion

No matter how harshly I might berate myself when I fumble, when it comes to my children's missteps, I aim to do the opposite. If it's an injury they've suffered because they were careless, I give them a hug and wipe their tears. If they perform poorly on a test because they haven't studied enough, I assure them they are not defined by one test, then calmly encourage them to think about what they might do differently next time. In each case, I offer gentle encouragement first, remind them that everyone makes mistakes, then explain that this is how we all learn. I ask them to remember this moment—the pain or sorrow or disappointment of it—and to grow from it so they'll be more careful, work a bit harder, and do better in the future.

Doing the same for myself is more challenging. At least, it used to be.

Most of us could not imagine speaking to another person as harshly as we speak to ourselves. And as we've seen, the self-scorn we dish out in our lowest moments has an impact, and it's rarely the one we are going for. We might believe, intuitively, that being tough on ourselves is helping in some way, like a parent who believes a spanking is for their child's own good. But berating ourselves isn't motivating, just as hitting a child isn't for their own good.

Why, then, do we beat ourselves up for skipping the gym, afraid that if we don't apply brute force, we'll never get there again? Why do we hate ourselves for occasionally overeating, procrastinating, exploding with anger, or mishandling a project at work—in other words, for being imperfectly human? Why are we cruel to ourselves in the aftermath, hoping once and for all to teach ourselves a lesson but only making things worse instead?

Could it be that we—that *you*—believe, as I once did, that the more you crack the whip against your own rump, the faster you'll run? Do you worry that acceptance might lead to passivity—even slothfulness—and that if you let yourself be content, you'll lose your edge and become complacent?

If so, you are not alone. According to research by Kristin Neff of the University of Texas, that fear of becoming complacent is the number one reason people hold on to their negative self-talk. Yet Neff's work suggests that this logic is as outdated as those spankings. In fact, it is not self-abuse, but self-compassion that supports motiva-tion and positive change. Allow me to repeat that: *self-compassion supports motivation and positive change.*

Self-compassion, it turns out, is the foundation of resilience and self-worth.

By remembering to speak to yourself with the same understanding and supportive encouragement you would extend to a close friend or your child, you will feel less stressed, happier, more self-confident, and more resilient during tough times.

When we summon our self-compassion, we step out of our small, fearful perspectives into a wider and kinder reality that puts us at ease. Self-compassion allows us to feel less armored and more supported. From that place, it's easier to face whatever needs facing and try again.

Learning to be more self-compassionate won't just help you feel better, it will also help you perform better. Rather than rendering you a contented couch potato, self-compassion acts as a springboard to greater success. The more you practice it, the more you will find, as I have, that kindness beats cruelty every time. As the research shows, it leads to a greater willingness to try and to accomplish big things.

Dr. Neff has developed several exercises to build self-compassion, all of which can be found at SelfCompassion.org. I've included one of my favorites below.

———

Exercise: Summon Self-Compassion

Step 1: Think about a situation in which a close friend is feeling badly or struggling in some way. How would you respond, especially when you're at your best? Write down what you'd typically do, what you'd say, and the tone in which you'd say it—the way you typically talk to your close friends when they're feeling down.

Step 2: Think about a time when you felt bad about yourself or were struggling. How do you typically respond to yourself in those situations? Write down what you typically do and say, and note the tone in which you talk to yourself.

Step 3: Did you notice a difference? If so, ask yourself why. What factors or fears come into play that lead you to treat yourself differently than others?

Step 4: How do you think things might change if, when you're suffering, you spoke to yourself in the same way you'd typically speak to a close friend?

Step 5: Start treating yourself just as you would a good friend and see what happens.

———

Exaggeration Elimination

Another simple tool that can help you channel self-compassion is something I call Exaggeration Elimination. It also happens to be solid gold when it comes to the not-so-kind stories you may tell yourself about other people. Before I go into it, though, I want to tell you about a friend of mine named Hannah. When I first met her, I was absolutely awed by all the colorful, fascinating, hilarious people she had in her life. Every weekend seemed to be a madcap adventure, and everyone she knew was "insanely brilliant," "drop-dead gorgeous," or notably fabulous in some way.

Then I happened to overhear her talking about *me* to some other friends, and I barely recognized the extraordinary version of the person she was going on about. I remember wishing that I did.

To Hannah's credit, her exaggerations were always over-the-top positive—well-meaning embellishments that cast her friends in the best possible light. They also made for better stories.

But the stories we tell ourselves about ourselves—or others, for that matter—are rarely so kind. Instead, our inner critics jump in with snide remarks or insulting labels. Take, for instance, the monikers we tend to assign to others—*The Flake, The Braggart, The Control Freak, The Jerk*. These are just a few of the painful labels that clients have used to describe their loved ones, and all too often, they see everything a person says or does through the lens of that label. *He is so unreliable. She is so full of herself. They are so selfish/controlling/critical/closed-minded.* After a while, it's as if they are no longer having a relationship with the actual person, but with their warped version of that person. And remember the negativity bias! These distorted versions of people are rarely as flattering as Hannah's.

Exaggeration Elimination asks you to recognize and name when you are thinking of someone in a biased, judgmental, unfair way and then replace that story with something more factual. For example, consider my client Marnie, a thirtysomething fashion merchandiser with a glamorous, globe-trotting lifestyle. "With my colleagues and friends," Marnie told me, "I feel capable, proud, and confident. But when it comes to my family—especially my infantilizing control freak of a mother—ugh!" Marnie complained of feeling babied and disrespected by her family, which then led her to lash out over petty, inconsequential things. More than anything, it was her mother's habit of texting frequent reminders about upcoming family plans, scheduling doctor appointments—even the need to write thank-you notes—that drove Marnie wild. From her perspective, her mother "had no faith in her," and Marnie viewed almost every reminder as "not just controlling, but totally insulting and proof of her disrespect." Seeing her mother through that lens, ironically, made Marnie so defensive that she behaved, in her words, "like a sullen and petulant child." Through our work, however, she learned to recognize this pattern and practice playing Exaggeration Elimination, which simply asked her to focus on the verifiable facts and details at hand instead of the larger "bad mother" story.

> **Fact:** My mother texted to remind me about my brother's birthday dinner.
> **Story:** My mother has no faith in me and thinks I am incapable of maintaining my own calendar.

Focusing less on our exaggerated stories and looking only at the facts—anything we can literally observe in the present situation—allows us to give others the benefit of the doubt so we can experience them more fully and connect more deeply. It helps us shift from a defensive or angry position to a more accepting and forgiving one, which, over time, can improve communication and deepen our bonds.

And that is no small matter.

Research confirms that social connections are really good for us, while loneliness is toxic. In fact, one of the longest-running studies on happiness, conducted by Harvard University for over seventy-five years, shows that healthy relationships boost longevity and overall well-being, perhaps more so than diet, exercise, quitting smoking, and even genetics.[19] Just as important, the same study also found that it's the quality of our relationships that matter more than the number of friends we have or whether or not we are in a committed romantic relationship. Having just one or two warm, positive relationships, it turns out, is protective of both body and brain.[20]

So, the next time you are tempted to berate your "flaky" sister because she is twenty minutes late for dinner, catch yourself and interrupt the pattern with Exaggeration Elimination.

Fact: My sister is late tonight.
Story: My sister *always* does this. She's selfish, immature, and disrespectful.

Next, broaden your thinking beyond your narrow, momentary judgment to think about the larger picture of who your sister really is. What other qualities does she possess? What do you love about her? What can you do with this extra bit of time that will be worth your while? (Is there something you can read as you wait? Might you benefit from a few quiet moments of solitude?)

Chances are, when she does show up, you will enjoy each other far more.

You can also use Exaggeration Elimination on yourself any time your inner critic is on the rampage. For example, recall a time when you realized you had made a mistake. Try to relive the moment of realization. What happens? How do you react? Maybe you get a spike of adrenaline that feels like poison coursing through your veins. Maybe your head begins spinning with excuses or justifications. Perhaps the thought of how stupid this is going to make you look, or how embarrassing it will be, makes your heart pound or your stomach lurch. Maybe your extremities get shaky and weak.

Then the inner critic jumps into the action.

As she begins lambasting you with insults, however, her focus is not on the present mistake, *but on your entire existence*. The problem isn't that you have *done something* arguably careless or stupid. It is that you *are* careless and stupid—and a whole lot of other cruel, awful things too.

This is where you want to play Exaggeration Elimination and separate the facts from the larger story.

Fact: You made an error.
Story: You are stupid and careless and can't do anything right.

Slightly exaggerated? I think so. In these moments, take some time to pause and breathe (I really can't say that enough!) and then parse the painful, sweeping distortions circling through your brain. Start by asking, "Is it true that I can't do *anything* right?" Then, as you did when you were playing lawyer, look at the evidence: you made a mistake; you sent an email you shouldn't have; you said something thoughtless. Notice how those isolated details pale in comparison to the dire drama of your over-the-top story.

As we've seen, our internal stories have a way of spiraling out of control. Learning to eliminate the exaggerated story by focusing on the facts—the actual details at play—will help you check your assumptions and remain present and calm (and far more capable of proceeding in a rational, effective way). Or, as Mark Twain once said, "Get your facts first, then you can distort them as you please."

The Three Ps

In moments of extreme disappointment or self-flagellation, practicing self-compassion can be incredibly healing. It is also the ultimate protective shield when your inner critic goes on the attack. For those of you who are exceptionally self-doubting or self-critical, I'd like to suggest a more proactive approach that will help you take your self-soothing one step further: a tool called the Three Ps.

The Three Ps represent your best traits—anything about yourself that is *positive*, *pride-worthy*, or *powerful*. I want you to start celebrating these attributes, your greatest strengths, every day. That's the tool, and you can use it while you're brushing your teeth, commuting to work, or at any time of your choosing. All you have to do is make a mental or written list of anything you appreciate about yourself: any skills and talents you possess, anything you've achieved or feel good about, anything at all that makes you feel proud, positive, or powerful.

Do this regularly, and you'll feel more confident over the long term, as the practice is intended to create and deepen a new, more emotionally supportive neural pathway in your brain, one your inner critic can't easily cross. As you do with the Win File, keep your list handy and refer to it whenever you need a boost.

If you're not quite feeling the Ps, author and motivational speaker Mel Robbins has a shortcut: Every morning, high-five yourself in the mirror. No pep talks, affirmations, or even speaking is required—just the high-five. A high-five signals recognition, support, and encouragement. It says: *I see you. I'm cheering you on, keep going, you've got this!* Whether we're high-fiving teammates on the field or strangers along a marathon route, it's a way of applauding effort, strength, and perseverance.

Why not give yourself some applause, too?

Permission Slip

What if you could write yourself a permission slip to just ignore all of the "shoulds" in your life: You "should" work harder; you "have to" put family first. Or maybe you believe you "owe" it to your children to remain in an unhappy marriage or that your obligation to maintain a certain career status "requires" you to tough it out in a soul-crushing job. Or perhaps you maintain relationships with people who drain your energy? Simultaneously, you might shy away from happier pursuits because you "shouldn't" or "can't" allow yourself to go there because of all those other obligations.

My point is that when it comes to caring for and prioritizing ourselves, the idea of permission often gets in the way. *Who do you think you are?* your inner critic demands. *Do you really have the right to say no to that and yes to this? Being an adult isn't meant to be all fun and games. Grow up and accept responsibility!*

Consider this permission slip an invitation to reflect on your values and honor your priorities. That might mean reorganizing your schedule or allowing yourself to say no to something you're dreading, even if it initially feels like an imperative. Or it might mean saying yes to something exciting or joyful, even when your inner critic views it as "unnecessary" or "frivolous" or "overly indulgent." Sometimes, it's simply checking in with your body and stepping away from the computer to stretch your aching back or get a glass of water.

When it comes to giving yourself permission, the first step, as always, is—say it with me—to pause. Then, clarify your goals and values. For so many of us, the conflict is often between work and play (or rest). We feel compelled to prioritize "responsibilities" over "indulgences" to put productivity and obligation ahead of pleasure and enjoyment. For others, the desire to challenge ourselves in new and exciting ways gets squelched, especially when taking a leap involves a risk of disappointing others or failing miserably and feeling like a fool. It's not that it's wrong to stay at your desk working on a beautiful day, even when your child asks you to go outside and play catch, but at least take the time to be mindful of your choices and motivations, identifying the *why* behind whatever you opt to do.

Next, think about the ways you tend to deny yourself permission. What stringent rules do you impose on yourself? What do you wish you could do more of, but continue to put off for another day because there's too much on your plate or because you believe you "can't" afford it? Have there been situations in the past where you didn't follow your inner knowing, but instead played by the "rules," then wound up regretting it? What lessons did you learn?

Finally, give yourself permission to honor your wants and desires rather than ignoring them. If you need to, write *Permission granted!* on a slip of paper and tape it to the wall over your desk. What works for me when I need permission is to think of my mom. She may be gone, but she remains my staunchest ally and greatest supporter, and losing her has allowed me a perspective that, when I summon it, always feels like permission.

Once you've granted yourself the freedom you deserve, choose with intention—perhaps after using the 3-D Approach from Chapter Ten. There is truly so much power in giving yourself choices rather than feeling like a victim of circumstances.

EIGHTEEN

Making Peace with Your Inner Critic

 Knowledge is of no value unless you put it into practice.

Anton Chekhov

NOT SO LONG AGO, I GOT INTO A HEATED DISCUSSION WITH MY daughter, Layla. She was fifteen at the time, a freshman in high school, and we were in the midst of the pandemic. Her classes had gone entirely online, and she was coping with the situation as well as could be expected, but I was worried about her and the amount of time she was spending alone in her room. When she came down to the kitchen one afternoon to grab a snack, I seized on the opportunity to try to connect. I started with benign chitchat, but before I knew it, I had said something—I have no idea what—that sent my girl stomping back up the stairs.

My impulse was to storm up there after her and demand that she pay me some respect and finish the conversation. Instead, I stayed put, inhaling and exhaling until I calmed down, assuring myself that I needed to give us both some time and space before revisiting the conversation.

When I found Layla in her room half an hour later, hunched

over her laptop amidst a stack of dirty dishes and laundry, I summoned my breath again and chose to ignore the mess.

"Can we talk?" I asked. "I'm worried about you," I confessed, in the kindest, most caring voice I could muster.

"All you ever do is criticize me," she shot back, her voice quivering with hurt more than anger. "I am such a good kid. I study and do well in school and stay out of trouble. But all you do is focus on my faults."

Reader, I was stunned.

The temptation was to argue back, to defend myself and point out all the ways her accusation was not only false, but preposterous.

All I do is criticize her?

This is entirely untrue! In fact, I rarely criticize her.

I *do* point out areas for improvement when I see them, but sparingly, and always gently. I am all too aware of Lola, who happens to sound just like my dad did, not to mention my clients, many of whom struggle with critical inner voices that remind them of their own parents. I make every effort to avoid being that voice for my children.

Or so I thought.

I continued breathing, my hand on my daughter's back, purposely holding my tongue even as my head spun with counterarguments. *How many times have I told you how proud I am of you, how proud you should be of yourself? How many times have I reminded you that everyone feels insecure at times, but that you should know how truly amazing you are?* "You've got it all," is what I often tell her, in fact.

All I do is criticize her?

Still breathing intentionally, I began to feel myself settle. It occurred to me that it did not matter who was right or wrong here. Layla was hurt. She *felt* criticized. That was her interpretation of whatever I said, the filter through which she received my comments. I know that filter well. No matter how innocently the words are delivered, they land sharply and painfully.

Layla was telling me how she felt, something I've long encouraged her to do. I want her to form her own opinions and be unafraid of expressing them. And wasn't this just Layla's negativity bias in action, her triggered brain ignoring the history of compliments, focusing only on the perceived slight? I didn't need to defend myself, I decided. I just needed to listen and try to repair the damage.

At that realization, I softened. The defensive arguments gave way to a feeling of tenderness—toward Layla, but also toward myself, my father … really, all of us! How vulnerable we are. How easily we feel hurt by one another.

I took another deep breath and apologized. I said I was truly sorry if anything I had said made her feel judged. I reminded her of how I really felt about her and expressed regret if I hadn't done enough to convey that lately. Eventually, we hugged and then went downstairs to join the rest of the family for a movie. Snuggled on the sofa, sharing a blanket and a bowl of popcorn, it occurred to me how differently this conversation could have gone if I'd stormed right up there after her without taking time to pause. My lawyerly nature, after all, is to argue and defend, to prove my point. And as much as I love my children and want them to know and feel it, I see my role much the way I imagine Lola sees hers. My job, first and foremost, is to keep them safe, to protect them from a harsh world, and to make sure they have the skills to succeed. This means love and tenderness sometimes take a backseat to more primal instincts. With Layla's head resting against mine, I was again grateful for my coach training, for the ability to check those harsher impulses and proceed with caution and compassion. There have been plenty of incidents where I couldn't quite manage it, and they didn't end with popcorn and snuggles.

———

BEING HUMAN IS MESSY, unpredictable, and decidedly imperfect. Misunderstandings will happen. I can say one thing, and Layla might hear something else entirely. Her negativity bias blocks out years of my support and encouragement as her survival instincts rear up, creating a story that says, "All I do," is criticize her. Our inner critics do like to generalize and exaggerate!

And all of us do this. All the time.

But just imagine if we didn't. By pausing and breathing, watching and questioning our thoughts, listening to our bodies, checking our inner critics, honoring our inner knowing, and practicing self-compassion, we open a world of possibilities.

I discovered this myself, as I continue to discover over and over again, when I recently ran my first half-marathon.

Prior to that race, I had never run more than five miles at a time. While I've embraced practically every fitness craze from step aerobics to kickboxing to Zumba to Spinning, going for a run was never my thing. To be honest, it felt like torture. Yet as I stood on the sidelines during the annual New York City Marathon, cheering on friends and total strangers, admiring their grit and stamina, I felt awed but also…envious. I desperately wanted one of those metallic body-warming blankets of my own (not to mention a medal!) but running 26.2 miles felt "impossible." By the time I hit my late forties, it seemed the opportunity had passed, and marathon glory would never be mine.

So, when my friend Laura asked me to run a half-marathon with her, my immediate reaction was "Hell, no!" She seemed surprised, given my love of exercise. "I'm just not a runner," I explained. (There's that labeling again!)

But Laura must have sensed some yearning in my voice, because she encouraged me to think about it. To my surprise, I told her I would.

The next day, I went for a trial run. Approximately ten minutes in, Lola showed up, and I felt a heavy reluctance spreading through my body. The feeling was familiar, but something I had always attributed to the act of running itself, as opposed to any negative stories in my head.

Then I remembered: perhaps I might benefit from observing and questioning my thoughts?

Don't be ridiculous, Lola scolded me. *This isn't about thoughts or beliefs. This is about running. You don't like it. It's too hard. It hurts. It's boring. You don't need this. Running sucks! In fact, you can't do it, so YOU suck!*

Our tendency is to receive the inner critic's familiar mental blather as the truth. Typically, that's what I would have done, allowing the negativity to weigh me down throughout the run, or stop me altogether. This time, instead of succumbing to Lola's same old unsupportive narrative, I decided to experiment with some thought work. What if this deeply ingrained "I hate running" story was the real source of my discomfort and agitation, rather than the activity itself?

I tested my theory by asking myself, *Is it true that I hate running? When I believe that thought, what happens?* Just by asking those questions, some of the strain I had always associated with the activity began to ease. Telling myself that I hated running—then doing it anyway—put me in conflict with myself. It triggered my telltale fight-flight-freeze response, making me feel tormented and indignant, sluggish and pained. *But who would I be without my story?* Just a woman out running, putting one foot in front of the other, lighter and freer, less burdened and hassled. Feeling emboldened, I wondered whether I could come up with examples to support the notion that I did *not* hate running, that I might even like it? This is where a big smile took over, and I exploded into laughter. The evidence was rather obvious. There I was. Running. Voluntarily. *Could I really hate it?* At that, I immediately felt a little extra pep in my step, something that has stayed with me on most running excursions since. Simply *pausing* to *observe, question,* and *reflect* on my limiting story around running allowed me to shift my perspective, adding palpable zeal to something that once felt like drudgery. My experiment felt like personal proof that the mind and body are intimately connected, demonstrating how our thinking can take a definite physical toll. But by questioning my story and doing away with the old attitude, I experienced a measurable physical boost that allowed me to run longer than I ever had before, and to enjoy the process.

From there, I identified other mental stories related to running that fell away just as easily. I dropped long-held notions about speed and stamina, about the "failure" of covering less ground than planned, or the "triumph" of adding more. In each case, shedding the stories left me feeling genuinely eager to *just* hit the trail and see where it led, rather than burdening myself with my old competitive tendencies and perfectionist thinking.

When I told Laura I would run the half-marathon with her, I was far from sure I could complete the race. But after performing my thought experiment, I took a more open "let's try and see" approach. I started with a five-mile run that felt pretty good. A few days later, I tried six, then eight, and a few days after that, ten.

Then I hurt my back.

This is where listening to my body became key. With about ten days left to train, sitting around nursing my back for a week was not what I had planned. In my former life, I would have loaded up on ibuprofen and forced it. (I say this with certainty because this is exactly what I did the last time I hurt my back, ignoring the pain and refusing to ease up on my workout routine, which ultimately left me sidelined and in agony for months.)

Fortunately, I have learned a few things since.

I laid off running and got the rest I needed. Rather than grumble about my aging body or bad luck, I flipped those negative thoughts to gratitude for all that I could do and for the healing time I had before the big day. I summoned self-compassion and nurtured my body. I took hot baths, visited a physical therapist, and stretched a lot (despite Lola insisting this was all "shamefully indulgent"). When I slipped into frustration or worry, I used R.A.I.N., *recognizing* and *allowing* the feelings, *investigating* the stories, and offering myself some *nurturing* and care.

When the morning of the half-marathon arrived, I still wasn't sure I could do it. But I told myself I would listen to my body and do my best. I would walk if need be or stop altogether, and there would be no shame in that. Lola would not be a spectator to this race.

Two hours and four minutes later, arms thrust upward in the international sign of victory, I crossed the finish line. And in the days and weeks that followed, with friends and family applauding my achievement, I was repeatedly struck by one thought: *these coaching tools really work.* Far more than self-discipline or even physical training, I can say with absolute certainty that my tools are what got me through the half-marathon experience—and a whole lot of other things, too.

———

IF THERE WAS one thing Martha Beck tried to instill in us throughout life coach training, it was this: *Live it to give it.*

Like the conscientious student I've always been, I have diligently followed this advice, integrating the tools and strategies I've shared in this book into my own life. That is how I can say with absolute confidence that you *can* overcome your painful personal patterns and your penchant for self-criticism. Use the methods we've explored. Employ the fourth C—*continue*—and practice them regularly. Remember to think twice, clarifying and confronting discouraging thoughts. Listen to your body and trust in its wisdom. Honor your inner knowing and use the 3-D Approach to feel more agency in your life. And please, cherish your relationships, extending kindness and compassion to yourself and others, too.

But if you take away only one thing from reading these pages, remember, first and always, to pause. Do it often. Pick out moments throughout the day—perhaps after a question from your spouse, a request from a colleague or a text from a friend—and use them as opportunities to delay your reaction time. Take a beat, a breath, and slow down. Be deliberate and intentional in your behavior and response, aiming to act from a relaxed, thoughtful state as opposed to one that is automatic or mindless. Practice pausing and breathing during ordinary exchanges, too, so you are more likely to do the same in heated or challenging moments.

The truth is, whatever the trigger, whether a hurtful comment from your partner or a scolding from your inner critic, we rarely need to react immediately. That's a good thing, because I guarantee that given a chance to reflect, a knee-jerk, instinctive reaction is almost never the one you would deliberately *choose*.

Is pausing contrary to our wiring? Absolutely. Hence the need for repetition and practice, for bolstering the circuitry that allows us to *choose* rather than succumbing to our more readily available instinct to see the negative and fight, flee, or freeze.

Those harsher instincts may never disappear, but over time, they will soften. All that pausing generates awareness, which creates opportunities to get curious. Whenever you notice your own telltale signs of stress, aggravation, frustration, and all the rest, you can begin to ask questions, starting with "why?" And once you've identified the trigger, you can pull out your tools and ask some additional questions. Whether you choose The Work, R.A.I.N., Exaggeration Elimination, or Cross-Examining the Witness, be proactive and deliberate about your self-questioning. And please remember to extend some compassion to yourself in the process.

Oh, and one more thing. Your inner critic deserves your compassion too. Remember, the problem isn't having a fearful inner voice; it's allowing that voice to take the reins and run you ragged. Like any intimate but fraught relationship, the trick is to accept your critic for who she is—an important part of you—but also to maintain your boundaries.

To do that, I suggest picturing your inner critic as a lifelong but difficult friend. Maybe you once hung on her every word, but over the years, you've evolved in ways that she has not. You know that in her own inelegant way, she wants what is best for you. So when she shows up—agitated, angry, and frightened—pause and be present. If necessary, let her have her tantrum; like all of our thoughts and feelings, her diatribe is unlikely to last very long before it fades away. Just remember to breathe, then hear her out, validating her feelings. Be tolerant and patient, but not deferential. Summon some compassion for your troubled friend, knowing that inner critic outbursts are usually well intended, albeit misguided. Try to smile as you thank her for her concern and offer her some reassurance. Then remind her that you are a mature and capable grown-up, that you've got the situation under control and that you don't need her help at this moment.

Whenever Lola arrives in my life now, this is exactly what I try to do. In fact, I take it one step further, reminding myself that our power dynamic has shifted. These days, I try to treat her more like a scared child awoken by a nightmare than an intimidating boss I must obey.

"Lola, is that you?" I might ask. "What's wrong? Why are you here? What do you need?"

From there, I conduct an internal investigation. What is she trying to protect me from? What was I doing, or thinking about doing, that got her attention?

Then I pull out whatever tool feels appropriate to do whatever work needs doing. Always, I start with deep breathing, calming myself down so that I can make any necessary decisions from a more responsive, clearheaded place. I tell myself an alternative story. Then I go on with my day.

I sincerely hope I've convinced you to try the same.

Afterword

Reader, I have a confession to make. The book you've just read wasn't the one I set out to write. That's because too often, the warring factions of my personality were at odds, with part of me pulled to offer something earnest and encouraging, while the other part (that would be Lola) attacking those instincts for being "cheesy" and "too soft," not to mention "common" and "embarrassing." Lola desperately wanted me to keep myself out of the story, mainly because "a real professional" would draw more from client examples and scientific evidence than personal anecdotes. I suspect there was also a lot of fear of failure tied up in that, too, combined with a life-long strategy of avoiding exposure and vulnerability. Above all, Lola frequently insisted that I lacked the legitimacy or authority to call myself an author and repeatedly sent me back to the bookstore to bone up on what the "actual experts" had to say. (Remember Tara Mohr's hallmark characteristics of the inner critic?)

So, after completing what I thought was the final draft, I put the manuscript into a drawer and told myself that I sucked as a writer and should stick with my day job.

And yet.

Almost daily, I found myself having conversations that made me think about my abandoned manuscript, and how the tools it contained might be able to help the friend or client I was talking to. Still, I didn't do anything about it until a client named Todd came into my life. During our initial consult, Todd told me that he needed help getting "happy," that he had all the ingredients in place—a fantastic wife, a fulfilling career, a daughter recently married to the love of her life—but he still felt plagued by a "vague heaviness," something "old and familiar, stubborn and dark." Todd had just turned sixty and was feeling his mortality. His goal, he told me, was to feel "lighter and brighter" and learn to better enjoy all the good things he had worked so hard to achieve.

It turns out that Todd's inner critic, whom he named Bruiser, was a lot like Lola, only meaner. Todd had grown up the youngest of four rough-housing brothers. His mother and father were largely absent and seemingly incapable of affection. Worse, Todd, as the runt of the litter, was picked on, neglected, relentlessly teased, and occasionally abused by his brothers. "Everything I have achieved," he told me, "has been a 'fuck you' to my family," his attempt to prove his worthiness. Now, he just needed to convince himself.

Todd, like many people I meet, had so much to offer this aching world. In his case, he worked with troubled teens and their families, helping them find the support and resources they needed to overcome their problems. Yet he felt himself plodding through his days, battling something he couldn't quite name. Together, we used the tools I've described in these pages to help him *pause, observe, question,* and *reflect,* going beyond the circumstances of his present life to the thoughts circling in his head. Because Todd was ready, we were able to make fast progress. Bruiser, whom we named in our second session, was as tough on Todd as his family had been. Not surprisingly, Todd's (i.e., Bruiser's) Greatest Hits were loaded with insults: *You're stupid. You're not worthy of your clients' trust. You have to work three times as hard to accomplish just enough. You can never let up. You have to keep proving yourself.*

No wonder he had such difficulty relaxing and enjoying life.

Over time, however, Todd learned to spot Bruiser's presence more quickly, recognizing when negative thoughts were driving his mood and behavior. By collecting his data, he came to see how many aspects of his current life—from the way he approached clients and colleagues to the way he felt on the golf course—were connected to an old set of beliefs and defensive strategies that *originally* served to protect or propel him, but once reexamined, no longer made any sense. Ultimately, with lots of practice, he was able to summon self-compassion when he felt overwhelmed, to pause and think twice and give himself the leeway, support, and soothing he needed to overcome his tendencies toward self-punishment.

None of this surprised me, since I know how well these tools work. What *did* surprise me was the extent to which my work with Todd helped me gain new insights into my own journey—both the progress and the detours. Along the way, I ended up learning as much from Todd as he was learning from me. As he showed up each week, courageously confronting Bruiser and the lifetime of self-doubting stories he represented, I couldn't help but recognize Lola's influence in my reluctance to share my writing. She was wily enough to vary the playlist, her tone softer, her warnings gentler and more reasonable than in the past. But she had me as tied up as ever with my old "You're not a real writer" story. And all of this made perfect sense, of course, as nothing stirs an inner critic like reaching for a big goal and exposing yourself to potential failure, with all the vulnerability that requires.

Just as Bruiser had no concern for Todd's happiness, Lola had no interest in my personal or professional growth, or even my desire to help others. Instead, like all inner critics, she only wanted to keep me safe. And so, Lola kept telling me that I'd better forget the book and "stay in my lane." Meanwhile, every day, I was meeting people who thought they were the only ones mired in self-doubt and self-criticism, just as I'd once believed. *Could it be that my book might help them?* And so, I returned to my tools once again, going beneath the negative thoughts, one at a time, *pausing, observing,* and *questioning,* then connecting the dots between my beliefs and my behavior, methodically challenging Lola's unhelpful criticism until my courage returned.

Remember back in Chapter Three, when I encouraged you to

identify your *whys*, assuring you that those deeper motivations could prove useful when the going gets rough? I was speaking from personal experience. Ultimately, it was my list of *whys*—my passion for helping people, my interest in sharing useful information, and my desire to connect meaningfully with others—that allowed me to stay the course. As it turns out, those values mean more to me than preserving the status quo or remaining safely anonymous. As a bonus, this entire experience has helped solidify my faith in these tools, reminding me that when we shed our self-directed negativity and learn to embrace our whole selves, flaws and all, we can unlock a whole world of change.

When we turn inward with compassion instead of judgment and kindness instead of hostility, we become more solid and self-assured, more comfortable in our skin and in our wider surroundings. The positive feelings lend themselves to generosity, creativity, possibility, and inspired action. And, from there, a new cycle can take hold, one where there is no need to attack ourselves—or anyone else, only to share the progress, the light, and the love.

I want to live in that world. Do you?

Acknowledgments

This book would not exist without the guidance, support, and love of many people, and I am deeply grateful to each one of you.

To Martha Beck—thank you for opening my eyes to an entirely new way of being in the world. Your wisdom, combined with your playful approach to both coaching and understanding the human condition, has transformed my life in countless ways. I will be forever grateful to you and the entire team at MBI for your dynamic, eclectic, and endlessly creative teachings. You inspired me to expand my perspective, and in doing so, you've helped me grow not only as a coach, but also as a person.

To my incredible clients, thank you for your trust and confidence, and for allowing me to share your stories. Most importantly, thank you for allowing me to share in your lives. It is a privilege I do not take lightly. I only hope I have been as helpful to you, as you have to me. You have each taught me more than you'll ever know.

I am forever grateful to Nicole Fouche, Jennifer Maurer, Betsy Slocum, Carolyn Carney, Lisa Lindberg, and Anne Hollows—"The Magical Moms"—without whom, I would not be half the coach I am today. At my most skeptical moments in training, you helped me stay the course and learn to trust in our new tools. Because of you, I discovered the meaning of "holding space," the power of vulnerability, and the value of embracing my whole self, woo-woo and all.

A heartfelt thanks to my early readers—Lisa Cornelio, Stephanie Town, Jennifer Singleton, Jamie Spannhake, Lisa Berg, Kate McCormick, Nicole Mersky, Jenny Harris, Jim Kelly, Maria Campbell, Sarah Payne, and Marla Saben. You are all very busy people, but you each made time for me and my manuscript at critical points along the way. Your thoughtful feedback, insightful suggestions, and unwavering enthusiasm for this project kept me moving forward, even when I wanted to give up.

My deepest appreciation to my team of editors—Molly Shulman, Paula Derrow, Marli Higa, and Deborah Kevin. I learned so much from each one of you, and thoroughly enjoyed the process. Your keen insights, expert guidance, and dedication to craft helped shape this book into something I could feel proud of. Thank you for sharing your gifts with me. I would never have come this far without you.

Special thanks to Lisa Garrigues for being an inspiring teacher, a gatherer of extraordinary women, and a guiding light. At a time when I felt unsure, impatient, and full of self-doubt, your writing classes were the bright spot in my week. Not only did you help me appreciate that there are many ways to be a writer, but you modeled the kind of woman I aspired to be when I grew up.

I am beyond blessed to have an abundance of kind, supportive, remarkable friends in my life. Luckily, there are too many of you to name, though I really wish I could! Whether we bonded back in New Ro, Kent, Ann Arbor, Tel Aviv, New York City, or Washington, you are the "Phone a Friend" people I can always count on. A special shout-out to The Brabies because you are my "of sisters"— you pick me up when I am down, make me laugh until I cry, and life would be so much duller without you.

To my parents, Leah and Michael, wherever you are—thank you for being exactly who you were. Everything I have, everything I've achieved, and everything I am is because of you. The foundation you laid, the lessons you instilled, and the love you gave have continued to shape my life long after you took your last breaths, and they always will.

To Martin—you have always been my steady presence in this unpredictable life, and I am so grateful to have you as a brother. From your laugh to your giant bear hugs to your inappropriate jokes, being with you always feels like home. I'm so proud of all that you've become. Forgive me for swindling you out of your room, and please visit me more often!

Huge thanks to my husband, Rob, my rock. Nothing about this beautiful life would or could exist without you. There's simply no one else I could have shared forever with. Thank you for your boundless love and support, for taking over the cooking so I could write, and for always believing in me. Thank you for coming up with a great title, too! I love you more each year.

To my children, Layla, Michael, and Summer—mothering you is pure joy. I don't know what I ever did to deserve the three of you, but not a day goes by that I am not grateful. Thank you for being sweet, affectionate, and funny. Thank you for keeping me grounded in my essential self, for bringing me "home" again, and for reminding me of the beauty of unconditional love. Please remember to play "Favorite Things" each night, to always believe in yourselves, and to love each other fiercely. And no matter what, remember this: you could never suck.

Resources

The following resources have been invaluable to me in learning to combat my penchant for self-criticism, and I trust they will be for you as well.

Books

Ahlers, Amy and Christine Arylo. *Reform Your Inner Mean Girl: 7 Steps to Stop Bullying Yourself and Start Loving Yourself*, Atria Books/Beyond Words, 2015.

Beck, Martha. *The Way of Integrity: Finding the Path to Your True Self*, Penguin Life, 2021.

Beck, Martha. *Finding Your North Star: Claiming the Life You Were Meant to Live*, Harmony Books, 2001.

Beck, Martha. *Steering by Starlight: The Science and Magic of Finding Your Destiny*, Rodale Books, 2008.

Beck, Martha. *The Joy Diet: 10 Steps to a Happier Life*, Piatkus Books, 2000.

Ben-Shahar, Tal. *Happier: Learn the Secrets to Daily Joy and Lasting Fulfillment*, McGraw-Hill, 2007.

Bernstein, Gabrielle. *Happy Days: The Guided Path from Trauma to Profound Freedom and Inner Peace*. Hay House, Inc, 2022.

Brach, Tara. *Radical Acceptance: Embracing Your Life with the Heart of a Buddha*, Random House Publishing Group, 2003.

Brown, Brené. *Daring Greatly: How the Courage to Be Vulnerable Transforms the Way We Live, Love, Parent, and Lead*, Avery Publishing Group, 2012.

Brown, Brené. *The Gifts of Imperfection: Let Go of Who You Think You're Supposed to Be and Embrace Who You Are*, Hazelden Publishing, 2010.

Brown, Brené. *Rising Strong: How the Ability to Reset Transforms the Way We Live, Love, Parent, and Lead*, Random House Publishing Group, 2015.

Chodron, Pema. *When Things Fall Apart: Heart Advice for Difficult Times*, Shambhala Publications, 1996.

Coelho, Paulo. *The Alchemist* (25th Anniversary Edition), HarperOne/HarperCollins, 2014.

Cope, Stephen. *The Great Work of Your Life: A Guide for the Journey to Your True Calling*, Bantam Books, 2012.

Csikszentmihalyi, Mihaly. *Flow: The Psychology of Optimal Experience*, Harper Perennial Modern Classics, 2008.

Duhigg, Charles. *The Power of Habit: Why We Do What We Do in Life and Business*, Random House, 2012.

Gallwey, Timothy. *The Inner Game of Tennis: The Classic Guide to the Mental Side of Peak Performance*, Random House, originally published 1974.

Gilbert, Daniel. *Stumbling on Happiness*, Knopf, 2006.

Goleman, Daniel. *Emotional Intelligence: Why It Can Matter More than IQ*, Bantam Books, 1995.

Hahn, Thich Nhat. *How to Love*, Parallax Press, 2015.

Helgesen, Sally and Marshall Goldsmith. *How Women Rise: Break the Twelve Habits Holding You Back*, Hachette Books, 2018.

Kaplan, Janice. *The Gratitude Diaries: How a Year Looking on the Bright Side Can Transform Your Life*, Dutton, 2015.

Katie, Byron. *Loving What Is: Four Questions That Can Change Your Life*, Harmony, 2002.

Mohr, Tara. *Playing Big: Practical Wisdom for Women Who Want to Speak Up, Create, and Lead*, Penguin Random House, 2014.

Neff, Kristin. *Self-Compassion: The Proven Power of Being Kind to Yourself*, William Morrow Paperbacks, 2015.

Peck, Scott M. *The Road Less Traveled: A New Psychology of Love, Traditional Values, and Spiritual Growth* (25th Anniversary Edition), Touchstone, 2003; originally published by Simon & Schuster, 1978.

Shapiro, Dani. *Still Writing: The Perils and Pleasures of a Creative Life*, Atlantic Monthly Press, 2013.

Spannhake, Jamie. *The Lawyer, The Lion & The Laundry*, Attorney at Work, 2019.

Taylor, Jill Bolte. *Whole Brain Living: The Anatomy of Choice and the Four Characters That Drive Our Life*, Hay House, 2021.

Wood, Wendy. *Good Habits, Bad Habits: The Science of Making Positive Changes That Stick*, MacMillan Books, 2019.

Podcasts

Bernstein, Gabby, host. *Dear Gabby*. https://gabbybernstein.com/podcast/

Brach, Tara, host. *Tara Brach*. https://www.tarabrach.com/talks-audio-video/

Brown, Brené, host. *Unlocking Us*. (https://brenebrown.com/podcast-show/unlocking-us/)

Harris, Tristan and Aza Raskin, hosts. *Your Undivided Attention*, The Center for Humane Technology, https://www.humanetech.com/podcast

Morin, Amy, host. *The Verywell Mind Podcast with Amy Morin*. (https://www.verywellmind.com/the-verywell-mind-podcast-5113058)

Raz, Guy, host. *How I Built This*, NPR. (https://www.npr.org/series/490248027/how-i-built-this)

Santos, Laurie, host. *The Happiness Lab*, Pushkin Industries, https://www.happinesslab.fm

Tippett, Krista, host. *On Being with Krista Tippett*, (https://onbeing.org/series/podcast/)

Zomorodi, Manoush, host. *The Ted Radio Hour*, TED Conferences, https://www.npr.org/podcasts/510298/ted-radio-hour

Courses, Talks, Blogs, and Other Resources

Martha Beck's Life Coach Training Course (now called Wayfinder Coach Training).

Coursera's Foundations of Positive Psychology, offered by The University of Pennsylvania and Dr. Martin E.P. Seligman.

Coursera's Buddhism and Modern Psychology, offered by Princeton University and Professor Robert Wright.

Heart Alchemy Yoga, classes available on YouTube.

Waldinger, Robert. **"What Makes a Good Life? Lessons from the Longest Study on Happiness."** Filmed November 2015 at TEDxBeaconStreet, TED video, 12:47. https://www.ted.com/talks/robert_waldinger_what_makes_a_good_life_lessons_from_the_longest_study_on_happiness.

Brown, Brené. **"The Power of Vulnerability."** Filmed June 2010 at TEDxHouston. TED video, 20:49. https://www.ted.com/talks/brene_brown_the_power_of_vulnerability.

Achor, Shawn. **"The Happy Secret to Better Work."** Filmed February 2011 at TEDxBloomington. TED video, 12:21. Posted May 2011. https://www.ted.com/talks/shawn_achor_the_happy_secret_to_better_work.

Gilbert, Dan. **"The Surprising Science of Happiness."** Filmed February 2004 at TED2004. TED video, 21:16. Posted September 2006. https://www.ted.com/talks/dan_gilbert_the_surprising_science_of_happiness.

The Daily Calm and The Daily Trip, both available on the Calm app.

The Marginalian (formerly Brain Pickings), by Maria Popova. (https://www.themarginalian.org).

Endnotes

1. Lewis, Charlton T., PhD, and Charles Short, LLD. *A Latin Dictionary*, Clarendon Press, Oxford, 1879.
2. "How Many Thoughts Do We Have Each Day?" Newshub, July 19, 2020. https://www.newshub.co.nz/home/lifestyle/2020/07/new-study-reveals-just-how-many-thoughts-we-have-each-day.html#:~:text=If%20your%20brain%20feels%20like,and%20end%20of%20each%20thought.
3. "Brain Facts." Healthy Brains by Cleveland Clinic, May 11, 2020. https://healthybrains.org/brain-facts/.
4. Lyubomirsky, Sonja. *The How of Happiness: A Practical Guide to Getting The Life You Want*. London: Piatkus, 2013.
5. *Ibid.* Throughout *The How of Happiness*, Lyubomirsky demonstrates how happiness is achieved and sustained through intentional habit changes (including our thinking habits) even more than circumstantial changes. She explores practices—or "habits"—such as expressing gratitude, avoiding social comparisons, having a spiritual practice, and finding ways to give back to your

community as examples of the kind of volitional activities that boost well-being. After trying them all, I can personally attest to their mood-elevating powers and highly recommend you try them for yourself.

6. Mohr, Tara. *Playing Big: Practical Wisdom for Women Who Want to Speak Up, Create, and Lead.* New York: Avery, an imprint of Penguin Random House, 2015, p. 13.

7. For a simple yet thorough explanation of this process, please refer to Dr. Daniel Siegel's hand model of the brain, which is accessible on YouTube at https://www.youtube.com/watch?v=f-m2YcdMdFw&t=14s.

8. Goleman, Daniel. *Emotional Intelligence: Why It Can Matter More Thank IQ.* New York: Bantam Books, 1995, p. 114.

9. If you are interested in calibrating your body compass in the Martha Beck style, please go to my website, talfagincoaching.com/services, where I will walk you through it.

10. As a new coach, I sometimes struggled to convey all the wisdom I had learned to those less willing to hear it. My high-achieving, professional clientele was as guarded and cynical as I had once been, often recoiling at some of the tools that seemed too playful or touchy-feely. Of course, I completely understood! I knew that if I wanted to be effective, I had to meet them where they were, coaching in a way that was palatable and practical. Still, I wanted to "help the muggles see the magic!" The answer, it turned out, was often about *language*. For example, many corporate clients preferred the terms "ditch" and "delegate" to "bag" and "barter"—hence the change to this tool, which I have altered in name only. Martha Beck deserves full credit for its substance.

11. If you would like to learn more about this, I recommend reading *Learned Optimism: How To Change Your Mind and Your Life* by Martin E.P. Seligman, PhD (see Resources).

12. Goleman. *Emotional Intelligence,* p. 65.

13. Taylor, Jill Bolte. *Whole Brain Living: The Anatomy of Choice and the Four Characters that Drive Our Life*. Carlsbad, CA: Hay House, Inc, 2022.

14. Neff, Kristin. "The Chemicals of Care: How Self-Compassion Manifests in Our Bodies." Self-Compassion.org. https://self-compassion.org/blog/the-chemicals-of-care-how-self-compassion-manifests-in-our-bodies/.

15. *Ibid.*

16. Emmons, Robert A., and Michael E. McCullough. "Counting Blessings versus Burdens: An Experimental Investigation of Gratitude and Subjective Well-Being in Daily Life." *Journal of Personality and Social Psychology* 84, no. 2 (2003): p. 377–89. https://doi.org/10.1037//0022-3514.84.2.377.

17. A systematic review published in the *Journal of Consulting and Clinical Psychology* (2011) examined the effects of gratitude interventions on mental health outcomes. The review indicated that gratitude practices were associated with reduced symptoms of depression and anxiety and increased levels of subjective well-being. Another study published in the *Journal of Happiness Studies* (2013) revealed that individuals who engaged in gratitude exercises demonstrated higher emotional intelligence compared with those who did not, and research published in the *Journal of Positive Psychology* (2008) explored the effects of a gratitude intervention on forgiveness, finding that participants who engaged in a gratitude exercise were more likely to forgive others and experienced greater psychological well-being compared with those who did not.

18. Emmons and McCullough. "Counting Blessings," p. 377–89.

19. Waldinger, Robert. "What Makes a Good Life? Lessons from the Longest Study on Happiness." TED Talk.

https://www.ted.com/talks/robert_waldinger_what_makes_a_good_life_lessons_from_the_longest_study_on_happiness/transcript?subtitle=en.

20. *Ibid.* (I highly recommend watching this TED talk.)

About the Author

Photo credit: Lora Noyes

Tal Fagin, a former attorney and now certified life coach, helps high-achieving individuals break free from self-doubt and perfectionism. As a coach, she partners with clients to clarify, comprehend, and solve problems. Her style is compassionate and direct—a combination of personal cheerleader, compassionate friend, and wise wingwoman. She lives in Connecticut with her husband, Rob, their three remarkable children, and their faithful Golden Retriever. She loves yoga, meditation, hiking, tennis, and sweaty workouts, but her true passion is people. She appreciates nothing more than connecting deeply and meaningfully with others.

linkedin.com/in/tal-fagin
instagram.com/talfagin
facebook.com/talfagin

About the Publisher

Founded in 2019, Highlander Press is a vibrant, mid-sized publishing house dedicated to transforming the world through the power of words. We are deeply committed to diversity and bringing big ideas to the forefront. At Highlander Press, we help authors navigate the journey from initial concept through writing, editing, and publishing, culminating in the release of a book that not only fulfills a lifelong dream but also solidifies their expertise and boosts their confidence.

Join us in making a mark in the literary world, where your voice is heard, and your message has the power to change lives.

facebook.com/highlanderpress

instagram.com/highlanderpress

linkedin.com/highlanderpress

tiktok.com/@highlanderpress

www.ingramcontent.com/pod-product-compliance
Lightning Source LLC
LaVergne TN
LVHW060806270625
814711LV00014B/20